MW01575115

Muhlenberg College
Allentown, Pennsylvania

Written by Michelle Hein

*Edited by Kimberly Moore,
Carrie Petersen, and Jon Skindzier,*

Layout by Matt Hamman

*Additional contributions by Omid Gohari,
Christina Koshzow, Chris Mason, Joey Rahimi,
and Luke Skurman*

ISBN # 1-4274-0100-4
ISSN # 1551-0498
© Copyright 2006 College Prowler
All Rights Reserved
Printed in the U.S.A.
www.collegeprowler.com

Last updated 5/13/06

Special Thanks To: Babs Carryer, Andy Hannah, LaunchCyte, Tim O'Brien, Bob Sehlinger, Thomas Emerson, Andrew Skurman, Barbara Skurman, Bert Mann, Dave Lehman, Daniel Fayock, Chris Babyak, The Donald H. Jones Center for Entrepreneurship, Terry Slease, Jerry McGinnis, Bill Ecenberger, Idie McGinty, Kyle Russell, Jacque Zaremba, Larry Winderbaum, Roland Allen, Jon Reider, Team Evankovich, Lauren Varacalli, Abu Noaman, Mark Exler, Daniel Steinmeyer, Jared Cohon, Gabriela Oates, David Koegler, and Glen Meakem.

Bounce-Back Team: Kimmy Zafran, Jacie Caras, and Zach Weiss.

College Prowler®
5001 Baum Blvd.
Suite 750
Pittsburgh, PA 15213

Phone: 1-800-290-2682
Fax: 1-800-772-4972
E-mail: info@collegeprowler.com
Web Site: www.collegeprowler.com

College Prowler® is not sponsored by, affiliated with, or approved by the Muhlenberg College in any way.

College Prowler® strives faithfully to record its sources. As the reader understands, opinions, impressions, and experiences are necessarily personal and unique. Accordingly, there are, and can be, no guarantees of future satisfaction extended to the reader.

© Copyright 2006 College Prowler. All rights reserved. No part of this work may be reproduced or transmitted in any form or by any means, including but not limited to, photocopy, recording, or any information storage and retrieval systems, without the express written permission of College Prowler®.

How this all started...

When I was trying to find the perfect college, I used every resource that was available to me. I went online to visit school websites; I talked with my high school guidance counselor; I read book after book; I hired a private counselor. Sure, this was all very helpful, but nothing really told me what life was like at the schools I cared about. These sources weren't giving me enough information to be totally confident in my decision.

In all my research, there were only two ways to get the information I wanted.

The first was to physically visit the campuses and see if things were really how the brochures described them, but this was quite expensive and not always feasible. The second involved a missing ingredient: the students. Actually talking to a few students at those schools gave me a taste of the information that I needed so badly. The problem was that I wanted more but didn't have access to enough people.

In the end, I weighed my options and decided on a school that felt right and had a great academic reputation, but truth be told, the choice was still very much a crapshoot. I had done as much research as any other student, but was I 100 percent positive that I had picked the school of my dreams?

Absolutely not.

My dream in creating *College Prowler* was to build a resource that people can use with confidence. My own college search experience taught me the importance of gaining true insider insight; that's why the majority of this guide is composed of quotes from actual students. After all, shouldn't you hear about a school from the people who know it best?

I hope you enjoy reading this book as much as I've enjoyed putting it together. Tell me what you think when you get a chance. I'd love to hear your college selection stories.

Luke Skurman
CEO and Co-Founder
lukeskurman@collegeprowler.com

Welcome to College Prowler®

During the writing of College Prowler's guidebooks, we felt it was critical that our content was unbiased and unaffiliated with any college or university. We think it's important that our readers get honest information and a realistic impression of the student opinions on any campus—that's why if any aspect of a particular school is terrible, we (unlike a campus brochure) intend to publish it. While we do keep an eye out for the occasional extremist—the cheerleader or the cynic—we take pride in letting the students tell it like it is. We strive to create a book that's as representative as possible of each particular campus. Our books cover both the good and the bad, and whether the survey responses point to recurring trends or a variation in opinion, these sentiments are directly and proportionally expressed through our guides.

College Prowler guidebooks are in the hands of students throughout the entire process of their creation. Because you can't make student-written guides without the students, we have students at each campus who help write, randomly survey their peers, edit, layout, and perform accuracy checks on every book that we publish. From the very beginning, student writers gather the most up-to-date stats, facts, and inside information on their colleges. They fill each section with student quotes and summarize the findings in editorial reviews. In addition, each school receives a collection of letter grades (A through F) that reflect student opinion and help to represent contentment, prominence, or satisfaction for each of our 20 specific categories. Just as in grade school, the higher the mark the more content, more prominent, or more satisfied the students are with the particular category.

Once a book is written, additional students serve as editors and check for accuracy even more extensively. Our bounce-back team—a group of randomly selected students who have no involvement with the project—are asked to read over the material in order to help ensure that the book accurately expresses every aspect of the university and its students. This same process is applied to the 200-plus schools College Prowler currently covers. Each book is the result of endless student contributions, hundreds of pages of research and writing, and countless hours of hard work. All of this has led to the creation of a student information network that stretches across the nation to every school that we cover. It's no easy accomplishment, but it's the reason that our guides are such a great resource.

When reading our books and looking at our grades, keep in mind that every college is different and that the students who make up each school are not uniform—as a result, it is important to assess schools on a case-by-case basis. Because it's impossible to summarize an entire school with a single number or description, each book provides a dialogue, not a decision, that's made up of 20 different topics and hundreds of student quotes. In the end, we hope that this guide will serve as a valuable tool in your college selection process. Enjoy!

OMID GOHARI ○ CHRISTINA KOSHZOW ○ CHRIS MASON ○ JOEY RAHIMI ○ LUKE SKURMAN ○
The College Prowler Team

MUHLENBERG COLLEGE
Table of Contents

By the Numbers............................ **1**	Drug Scene................................ **90**
Academics **4**	Campus Strictness **94**
Local Atmosphere **11**	Parking.. **98**
Safety & Security **18**	Transportation **103**
Computers.................................. **22**	Weather.................................... **109**
Facilities...................................... **27**	Report Card Summary **113**
Campus Dining.......................... **33**	Overall Experience **114**
Off-Campus Dining **38**	The Inside Scoop..................... **118**
Campus Housing **47**	Finding a Job or Internship **123**
Off-Campus Housing................ **55**	Alumni **125**
Diversity..................................... **60**	Student Organizations............ **127**
Guys & Girls............................... **65**	The Best & Worst.................... **130**
Athletics...................................... **71**	Visiting...................................... **132**
Nightlife...................................... **77**	Words to Know....................... **138**
Greek Life **85**	

Introduction from the Author

When I first started telling people that I was going to be a student at Muhlenberg College, I typically found myself following up this response with an explanation of, "It's a small liberal-arts college in Allentown." I admit that I had never even heard of Muhlenberg until my best friend, now my college roommate, started telling me about the school and convinced me to attend an open house during our junior year of high school. It was during this initial visit that I fell in love with the friendly and welcoming campus that made me immediately feel like I wanted to call this place home for my four years of college. Years later, I have found that I need to use my explanation of Muhlenberg less and less as the college becomes increasingly more well known.

Over the past several years, Muhlenberg has been going through many changes that have contributed to the overall growth of the college. These changes make this an interesting time to be on campus, as you see them take place before you. While the school still prides itself on its small student to faculty ratio, the popularity of the college has been growing rapidly. Each year, the number of applicants has been increasing as more people are catching on to all of the opportunities that Muhlenberg has to offer. Some of the most visible changes have been the construction of new academic buildings, dormitories, art and theater facilities, and the renovation of the athletic center. It's exciting to see the college grow with its students while still maintaining the same warmth and integrity that it had in the beginning.

There is a mixture of students who come to Muhlenberg: those who know exactly what they plan on doing with the rest of their lives, like the students who come in pre-med, and those who aren't quite sure which direction they plan on going. What makes the academic experience at Muhlenberg so appealing is that it allows both of these types of people to be successful. The work is challenging; however, Muhlenberg students will tell you that the professors here are not only among the most knowledgeable in their field, but they are also extremely supportive. You will never become a number or just a face in the crowd. It is to this combination of academic excellence and personal attention that so many students attribute their decision to attend Muhlenberg.

It's impossible to completely grasp the feeling of community and warmth of Muhlenberg by reading a book, and not everyone experiences that immediate feeling the moment they step on campus like I did. This is why it's so important to ask yourself what you're looking for in a college and do your research. Hopefully, this book will help you in that process as you read what current students have to say about their experiences at the 'Berg.

Michelle Hein, Author
Muhlenberg College

By the Numbers

General Information

Muhlenberg College
2400 W Chew Street
Allentown, PA 18104-5586

Control:
Private

Academic Calendar:
Semester

Religious Affiliation:
Lutheran

Founded:
1848

Web Site:
www.muhlenberg.edu

Main Phone:
(484) 664-3100

Admissions Phone:
(484) 664-3200

Student Body

Full-Time Undergraduates:
2,242

Part-Time Undergraduates:
0

Total Male Undergraduates:
1,015

Total Female Undergraduates:
1,431

Admissions

Overall Acceptance Rate:
45%

Early Decision Acceptance Rate:
71%

Regular Decision Acceptance Rate:
42%

Total Applicants:
4,040

Total Acceptances:
1,808

Freshman Enrollment:
559

Yield (% of admitted students who actually enroll):
30%

Early Decision Available?
Yes

Early Action Available?
No

Total Early Decision Applicants:
448

Total Early Decision Acceptances:
299

Early Decision Deadline:
January 15

Early Decision Notification:
February 1

Regular Decision Deadline:
February 15

Regular Decision Notification:
March 15

Must Reply-By Date:
May 1

Applicants Placed on Waiting List:
1,306

Applicants Accepted from Waiting List:
476

Students Enrolled from Waiting List:
17

Transfer Applications Recieved:
86

Transfer Applications Accepted:
14

Transfer Students Enrolled:
12

Transfer Application Acceptance Rate:
16%

Common Application Accepted?
Yes

Supplemental Forms?
Only if applying for early decision or SAT optional plan

Admissions E-Mail:
admissions@muhlenberg.edu

Admissions Web Site:
www.muhlenberg.edu/admissions

SAT I or ACT Required?
Neither required

SAT I Range (25th–75th Percentile):
1120–1320

SAT I Verbal Range (25th–75th Percentile):
560–660

SAT I Math Range (25th–75th Percentile):
560–660

Retention Rate:
93%

Top 10% of High School Class:
43%

Application Fee:
$45

Financial Information

Tuition:
$28,760

Room and Board:
$7,270

Books and Supplies:
$1,000

Average Financial Aid Package (including loans, work-study, grants, and other sources):
$16,728

Students Who Applied for Financial Aid:
53%

Students Who Received Aid:
74%

Financial Aid Forms Deadline:
February 15

Financial Aid Phone:
(484) 664-3175

Financial Aid E-Mail:
finaid@muhlenberg.edu

Financial Aid Web Site:
www.muhlenberg.edu/finaid

Academics

The Lowdown On...
Academics

Degrees Awarded:
Associate
Bachelor

Most Popular Majors:
15% Social Sciences
14% Biology
14% Business, Marketing
9% Drama, Theater Arts
8% Psychology

Full-Time Faculty:
155

Faculty with Terminal Degree:
85%

Student-to-Faculty Ratio:
12:1

Average Course Load:
Four classes

Graduation Rates:
Four-Year: 76%
Five-Year: 81%
Six-Year: 82%

Cooperative Programs

3-2 or 4-2 combined-degree program in engineering (Columbia University or Washington University MC Penn Dental Program or University of Pennsylvania School of Dental Medicine), Lehigh Valley Hospital scholars (Drexel University College of Medicine and Lehigh Valley Hospital), seven year optometry program (State University of New York), 3-2 or 4-2 combined degree program in environmental science or forestry (School of the Environment at Duke University)

AP/IB Test Score Requirements

Possible credit and/or placement for scores of 3, 4, or 5

Best Places to Study

Martin Luther Underground, Trexler Library, Red Door

Sample Academic Clubs

Accounting Society, Biology Club, Communication Club, Education Society, Math Club, Physics Club, Psychology Club, Science Club, Spanish Club

Did You Know?

Many Muhlenberg students take advantage of study abroad programs. Muhlenberg has college affiliates in Argentina, Australia, Spain, China, Czech Republic, Denmark, Ecuador, England, France, Germany, Ireland, Italy, Japan, Netherlands, and Scotland. A semester in Washington DC is also an option.

If a student wishes to **study something that is not designated as a major**, that student has the option of proposing a self-designed major.

When coming to Muhlenberg, you may be asked to apply to one of the three different scholar programs on campus. These programs include Dana Associates, Muhlenberg Scholars, and RJ Fellows. Each program offers different opportunities for some of Muhlenberg's brightest and most talented students.

Muhlenberg's Office of Academic Support offers students many services, including an excellent peer tutoring program with over 200 trained peer tutors. Individual and small group tutoring are available on a weekly basis at no cost.

Muhlenberg College has set seven application records in the past few years.

Students Speak Out On...
Academics

> "The teachers at Muhlenberg are awesome for the most part. They are very helpful, and they love to get to know their students and challenge you in ways that are interesting."

Q "Some professors are really good at making meaningful presentations that keep students engaged and interested. Those are the professors I try to take again. Others are **just very boring**, and the hour and 15 minutes twice a week seems like an eternity. When I encounter those professors, I avoid taking classes with them again."

Q "The professors are amazing! They never miss an opportunity to hear your opinions, and any class can become a 'discussion class.' They never shy away from challenging the students; yet, they are **always available for extra help** or just for a good talk."

Q "The professors are phenomenal. The key is finding the professors you like and taking everything they offer. I find my classes very interesting and satisfying. **The syllabus is always scary**, but somehow, it becomes manageable because the classes are just so interesting."

Q "For the most part, I have found the professors to generally be nice people, but not necessarily good teachers. Most professors do seem **very willing to meet students outside of the classroom** for extra help, though. I can honestly say that I have learned at least one interesting thing from every class I have taken at Muhlenberg."

Q "The professors are wonderful; they are definitely one of the best things about Muhlenberg. You are able to make long-lasting connections with them. **Many professors even invite students to their homes** and give out their home phone numbers. The small classes and convenient office hours make it easy to get to know your professors and for them to get to know you. Professors care about students and respect them as intellectuals."

Q "The classes here can be difficult, but you don't come to a college like Muhlenberg to sit back and relax. You want to have fun, but **you also want to learn**. I feel like Muhlenberg has a great balance of both of those things."

Q "I had been advised to make an effort to get to know my professors. Before coming to Muhlenberg, I never realized how easy that could be. All of my professors have seemed **genuinely interested in my progress** in their classes and even outside of the classroom."

Q "At some schools, you can go through an entire semester without a professor even knowing your name. At Muhlenberg, **your professors will remember things about you** years after you take their class."

Q "One of the best parts of Muhlenberg is the enthusiasm coming from the professors. It makes going to class fun. You remain **a name rather than a number**. Some professors require you to call them by their first name because they're more like friends and mentors than lecturers."

Q "I know that my experiences with my professors have been totally different than experiences at other colleges. The professors at Muhlenberg go out of their way to get to know each student. They want to know what your life is like, and they want to help you in any way they can. **I never hesitate to go to my professors** with any questions I have, or sometimes, I go to them just to get some advice."

The College Prowler Take On...
Academics

Muhlenberg prides itself on its combination of strong academics and a caring community. Unlike some larger colleges, there are no teaching assistants who actually teach you the material you are responsible for knowing. Although there will obviously be a few professors who students don't like, the thing that stands out the most about Muhlenberg professors is how extremely accessible and personable they are. Most professors give out their home phone numbers on the first day of class, and you shouldn't be surprised if professors even invite you to their houses. Professors are eager to do anything they can to help you with a class by meeting with you during office hours or by appointment. A large majority of the professors live near the campus, and it is not unusual to see them in the city or around campus just hanging out or attending student events. Keep in mind that since the professors know their students well, they notice when you skip class or fall asleep. If you are looking for professors who will give you individual attention and genuinely care about your progress, you are in luck.

Along with this excellent personal support, Muhlenberg offers students a variety of academic opportunities. While Muhlenberg is known for its excellent pre-med program, it is also well known for theater and dance. It is this type of academic diversity that makes Muhlenberg a great place, not only to learn facts, but also to learn how to think and understand many different fields of learning.

The College Prowler® Grade on
Academics: B+

A high Academics grade generally indicates that professors are knowledgeable, accessible, and genuinely interested in their students' welfare. Other determining factors include class size, how well professors communicate, and whether or not classes are engaging.

www.collegeprowler.com

Local Atmosphere

The Lowdown On...
Local Atmosphere

Region:
Northeast

City, State:
Allentown, PA

Setting:
Medium-sized city

Distance from Philadelphia:
1 hour

Distance from New York:
1 hour, 30 minutes

Distance from Baltimore:
2 hours, 30 minutes

Points of Interest:
Allentown Art Museum
Allentown City Hall
Allentown Fairgrounds
Bear Creek Ski Area
Cedar Beach Park
Center Square
Crayola Factory
Dorney Park and Wild Water Kingdom
Haines Mill Museum
Historic Bethlehem
Lehigh County Museum
Liberty Bell Shrine
Nazareth Speedway
Trexler Game Preserve
Trexler Park

Closest Shopping Malls:
Lehigh Valley Mall
Shops at Cedar Point
Village West Shopping Center
Whitehall Mall

Closest Movie Theaters:
AMC Tilghman Square 8
4608 Broadway St., Allentown
(610) 391-0780

19th Street Film Series
527 N 19th St., Allentown
(610) 432-0888

Carmike 16
1700 Catasaqua Rd., Allentown
(610) 264-9624

Major Sports Teams:
76ers (basketball)
Eagles (football)
Flyers (hockey)
Phillies (baseball)

City Web Sites
www.allentownpa.org
www.city-data.com/city/Allentown-Pennsylvania.html

Did You Know?

5 Fun Facts about Allentown:

- Allentown is considered the "**truck capital of the world**."
- **A local church harbored the Liberty Bell** when it was taken from Philly to prevent British seizure.
- **The 1988 movie *Hairspray* was filmed in Allentown.**
- **Allentown was named after William Allen**, early landowner and son-in-law of Alexander Hamilton.
- While he grew up on Long Island, Billy Joel's song "Allentown" is a depiction of life in **industrial Allentown during the 1980s**.

Students Speak Out On...
Local Atmosphere

"There are a bunch of universities nearby. This is a great resource because you can go to other campuses to meet people or to get extra books for research."

Q "A lot of people complain that there is nothing to do in Allentown, but I only agree to an extent. There is a nearby mall and a good amount of restaurants, movie theaters, and coffee shops; however, for the student looking for active nightlife, Allentown is not the best place to go. Lehigh and Lafayette are relatively nearby, and many students take advantage of the **greater social opportunities**."

Q "**West Allentown is beautiful**. You feel classy walking through some of the neighborhoods on your way to rent videos or buy groceries. Trexler Park offers walking and biking paths, and the rose garden is an incredible place to visit for your photography class. Dorney Park is only about two miles away."

Q "Allentown can be a cool place, but **you have to know where to look** and find your own fun."

Q "This part of Allentown is very affluent; it has a very suburban feel to it. Cedar Crest College is right down the street, but they might as well be on the other side of the country because we really don't do anything with them cooperatively. **Try not to get lost and end up downtown** by yourself; it can be scary!"

Q "While you may not expect it, Allentown has **some great cultural sites**. Try to take a look at them because they can be a great alternative to the usual weekend happenings. Also, go to the parks! They are beautiful, and there are several within easy walking distance from campus. They can be great for some fun with friends or even for a new quiet place to study."

Q "Allentown is really cool if you explore everything you can. People make fun of Allentown and say it's boring, but it has most of the same things that other towns have. Unless you are familiar with downtown Allentown, I would not advise you to travel down there alone. It is a cool place, but **you should be cautious about exploring it**. Definitely check out 19th Street. Hava Java's is a really cool little coffee shop, and the 19th Street Theater has movies and shows throughout the year."

Q "The downtown area of **Allentown has a lot of poorer areas**, but it seems to have a bit more life. People tend not to be especially open-minded to it because it is labeled the 'sketchy area,' so there is a lot of complaining about nothing to do. I think if people took the time to look into some of the shops, parks, and restaurants, they'd be more satisfied, because some of the places have a little more character than typical suburban areas."

Q "The residential section just outside of the college is **nice for taking a walk in the fall or spring**. Woody's and Stooges are bars within walking distance that cater to students, and Wegmans is definitely worth frequent visits."

Q "I love going into the city to work with the children. There are **a lot of opportunities to volunteer** in the inner city, and the children always seem really happy to see us."

Q "Each year, I'm amazed by how much there is in Allentown that I never knew about. My first year here, I was kind of scared into staying on campus or only going to places like the mall and the movies. Now that I've become more relaxed about where I'm willing to go, I've realized that **the areas around campus have so much more to offer** than I initially thought."

Q "Some people actually seem scared to go into the city. It's not that bad! If you've ever been into cities like Philly or New York, Allentown is nothing. Sure, there are areas that are sketchier than others; yet, I really don't feel like they are too dangerous to explore them with your friends. Take some trips on the weekends just to **check out the places that are near campus**. You'll find that Allentown isn't as dangerous or as boring as you might think."

Q "Allentown has everything you would expect from a moderately-sized city: movie theaters, bars, dance clubs, restaurants, and shopping. **Some areas of Allentown are nicer than others**. The college itself is located in a very safe and pretty part of the city; however, it's close enough to the inner city to provide other opportunities."

The College Prowler Take On...
Local Atmosphere

Muhlenberg is located in the center of two different areas of Allentown. Off the west side of campus, you have the fairly wealthy side of Allentown that has a much more suburban feel to it. There are several shopping centers that provide some college necessities within walking distance such as grocery stores, beer distributors, pizza places, ice cream, movie rental, and pharmacies. If you're willing to get in the car, there is a 24-hour Wal-Mart within 10 minutes that is very useful for those random late-night snack runs. Going in that same direction, you pass Dorney Park. This is great during the beginning and end of the year because they have good prices at those times, and you can also get group discounts. In addition to the nice neighborhoods, there are also several parks nearby that are great for taking walks when thereis pleasant weather. Cedar Beach Park has a lot of ponds and streams with statues and fountains, and it is also where you can find the must-see rose garden.

If you head east of campus, you go into downtown Allentown. This is more of your typical city with some historic and cultural spots. A lot of students and most Muhlenberg freshmen get so trapped in the "Muhlenberg Bubble" that they don't give downtown Allentown a chance. In addition to having a lot of rewarding places to volunteer (such as an after school program called Casa Guadalupe), downtown also offers several social and cultural spots such as the Allentown Art Museum on 5th Street and the 19th Street Theater. There are five other colleges that are nearby and part of the Lehigh Valley Association of Independent Colleges (LVAIC). As a part of this association, Muhlenberg students are able to take classes and use the libraries at DeSales University, Lafayette College, Lehigh University, Moravian College, and Cedar Crest College.

The College Prowler® Grade on

Local Atmosphere: C+

A high Local Atmosphere grade indicates that the area surrounding campus is safe and scenic. Other factors include nearby attractions, proximity to other schools, and the town's attitude toward students.

Safety & Security

The Lowdown On...
Safety & Security

Number of Muhlenberg Police:
10

Muhlenberg Police Phone:
(484) 664-3110

Safety Services:
Crime prevention services
Emergency phones
Escort service
Operation identification
Rape Aggression Defense program

Health Services:
Basic medical services
Counseling services
Daily delivery services from outside pharmacies
Gynecological services through an appointment system
Pregnancy tests
Selected diagnostic studies

Health Center Office Hours:
Monday–Friday 8 a.m.–5 p.m.

Students Speak Out On...
Safety & Security

"I have walked home at all hours of the night, and I have never felt unsafe on campus. The campus is compact and very well lit. Campus safety is always patrolling on foot and by car."

Q "We have campus safety officers who are around campus and will provide students with an escort home from buildings if they feel unsafe. I feel safe on campus and have never used this service, but it's nice to know that it's available. There are **emergency call-boxes throughout campus** that have bright blue lights on them. If something happens to a student while they're walking on campus, they can press the button. Campus safety will respond and arrive at the call-box's location."

Q "I feel completely comfortable walking around campus by myself at night. **It's a very safe campus.**"

Q "I have always felt **very secure and safe on campus**. Campus safety is always around, and there isn't a great deal of violence or robbery on campus."

Q "The security and safety on campus is very good. **Campus police are always around** and roaming. Since the campus is so small, it is a very safe environment."

Q "I've never felt less than safe. You can always see campus safety driving around. Since **everyone is friendly and the student body is small**, the officers know you and you know them. That makes it easier to come to them if you have a problem."

Q "Security and safety is good, but **it's not overboard so that's nice**. I feel safe walking around alone at night, but I also appreciate that I don't have to go through tons of security measures to bring off-campus friends into my dorms. When you see what some other schools make you go through just to visit a friend in a dorm, it makes you happy that Muhlenberg is able to trust its students while keeping them safe."

Q "Overall, **Muhlenberg has a very safe campus**. I would feel comfortable walking almost anywhere on campus alone at night. If you don't for some reason, there is a service that can shuttle you around campus."

Q "**I feel safer walking around Muhlenberg** than I do in my own town."

Q "I think the campus security is amazing. They are very friendly people and committed to student safety, and they seem to be quite effective. Realistically, **we can't expect them to stop every crime** or danger, but they seem to do well."

Q "I feel like I see **campus police everywhere** I go. Sometimes, I even see them when I'm off Muhlenberg campus just driving around! At times, I think that's a little weird, but it's also nice to know that they're available if I ever did feel nervous about my surroundings."

The College Prowler Take On...
Safety & Security

Students at Muhlenberg agree that the campus is very safe. It is rare to hear of any crimes occurring on campus or in the immediate areas surrounding the campus. While most people would not recommend walking around parts of Allentown alone at night, even the most paranoid students feel comfortable walking anywhere on campus at any time. Just in case you do get worried, you can usually spot one of the campus safety vehicles or an officer on foot at most times of the day and night. You can even call campus safety and get someone to escort you to your room if you are really nervous. The emergency phones are also always readily available, as they are spread out all over campus. On the other side, it is also nice that security isn't overly strict either. While some schools have really inconvenient policies about having guests, Muhlenberg's security is more realistic and trusting of its students. Each dorm requires a student to use their ID to gain access to their building, but you do not need to go through any other security points. You are able to have guests, and you are only asked to register them if they are staying overnight.

Like all institutions with a large number of people, Muhlenberg is not immune to all cases of crime; however, the overall atmosphere of the campus is very safe. Most incidents that you hear about concern relatively minor acts of vandalism and are usually not a reason to become overly upset. The environment of a close community and the visible presence of campus safety combine to make Muhlenberg's campus a comfortable and secure place to live.

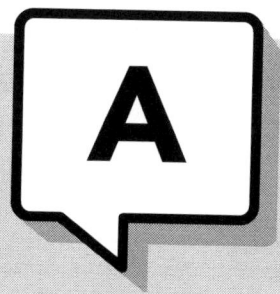

The College Prowler® Grade on
Safety & Security: A

A high grade in Safety & Security means that students generally feel safe, campus police are visible, blue-light phones and escort services are readily available, and safety precautions are not overly necessary.

Computers

The Lowdown On...
Computers

High-Speed Network?
Yes

Wireless Network?
Not yet (but they're working on it)

Number of Labs:
25

Number of Computers:
200+

Operating Systems:
Windows XP

Free Software:
McAfee AntiVirus

Discounted Software:
Microsoft OneNote 2003
Microsoft XP Pro Upgrade
Microsoft Office Pro 2003
Microsoft Office Standard 2003

24-Hour Labs:
Residence hall labs
Ettinger

Charge to Print?
No

Did You Know?

Muhlenberg computer labs are only equipped with PCs, not Macs.

The Office of Information Technology's (OIT) Student Help Desk is open seven days a week. It is located in the lower level of Ettinger.

Muhlenberg students are provided with free e-mail accounts their freshman year that they keep for all four years. Many professors and other members of the Muhlenberg faculty use these accounts to send important information to students, so make sure to check your e-mail regularly or have it forwarded to your other accounts.

Unlike some other colleges, Muhlenberg's OIT offers free computer assistance to its students. While computer problems are always stressful, at least you won't be paying to get the help you need!

Students Speak Out On...
Computers

> "Definitely bring your own computer. The computer labs are usually empty, but the printers never have paper. It is a lot easier just to have your own computer."

Q "The computer network works pretty well, though sometimes **it will crash and students can't get online** for a few hours. This is common on college campuses, though, since so many students are on the network at once. I would recommend bringing your own computer just because it can get annoying in the computer labs. Often, students working on group projects go in there to work, so it can get a bit loud. I never brought a printer to Muhlenberg, and I don't think it's necessary."

Q "With computers available in the library, Trumbower, Ettinger, Moyer, and every dorm, I would venture to guarantee that **there is always a vacant, nicely functioning computer on campus**. Of course, personal privacy, peace, and stillness are pretty crucial, so you should bring your own PC as well."

Q "There are computer labs, but the computers are not always in the greatest condition. **The printers are almost never working** in the labs in the dorms. I would recommend your own computer and printer. The labs are not usually crowded, but there is no guarantee that they will work very well."

Q "I get really frustrated with OIT (Office of Information Technology) because sometimes, **I have to wait days at a time for them to fix my computer**. Once I do get through and they help me out, they do so really efficiently, and I never really have problems with the network."

Q "OIT is very helpful, and they have fixed my computer on more than one occasion. **I would highly recommend bringing a computer** to campus. It is sometimes much easier to type in your room, without distraction, than in the computer lab, where it can be noisy."

Q "There are plenty of computer labs around campus, so you should always be able to find some space. The computers usually work decently, but the **printers are usually broken or out of paper**. I suggest bringing your own laptop. It's nice for small desks, going outside, and portability for group meetings."

Q "**The computer labs always have room**, but I would recommend bringing your own computer anyway because Instant Messenger is a pretty big deal. Also, it's easier to motivate yourself to do work if the computer is right there in your room instead of down the hall."

Q "The computer labs are pretty available, but **they can get crowded around finals**. I would absolutely bring your own computer because the Internet often becomes your connection to friends from home when you're in college."

Q "You should **bring your own computer** to any college because you will live on it! Laptop or desktop is a personal choice. Although I prefer desktops, laptops are nice because of their small size. You'll find you have much more space, and it's easier to move."

Q "I suggest bringing your own computer because college students live on Instant Messenger. Even at a small school like Muhlenberg, **people send Instant Messages to set up everything from weekend plans to study sessions**."

The College Prowler Take On...
Computers

Computers are a huge part of college life. As a result, there are very few students who do not bring their own computers. A lot of professors and student organizations will communicate through e-mail, so it is not unusual for students to check their e-mail compulsively, and all students are assigned Muhlenberg e-mail accounts as freshmen. Muhlenberg asks all students to have their computers registered to be part of their MuleNet. You will need to pay $65 to have this done, which causes complaints from many students because they find it unnecessary. You can find labs in the library, any of the dorms, and in several of the academic buildings. Since most students do have their own computers, there is hardly ever a problem finding an open computer. Free printing is also available in the labs, so many students will bring their own computer, but not a printer.

Opinions of OIT depend largely on personal experiences. Some people have great success stories of OIT saving them when they've had computer problems, while others will tell you that the staff was totally unhelpful. Muhlenberg's technology is top notch in some areas, but there are other areas that students have complaints about. You can always find an open computer to work on, but some of the computers can be really slow. It is free to use the printers, but they are often out of paper. In general, students are pleased with the Internet connection. This is important to college students since so much communication is done through the Internet. Muhlenberg has not gone wireless yet, but it's something that they are talking about for the future.

The College Prowler® Grade on
Computers: B-

A high grade in Computers designates that computer labs are available, the computer network is easily accessible, and the campus' computing technology is up-to-date.

Facilities

The Lowdown On...
Facilities

Student Center:
Seegers Union

Athletic Center:
Life Sports Center

Library:
Trexler Library

Campus Size:
75 acres

Popular Places to Chill:
General's Quarters (GQ)
The Lawn
Parents Plaza
Red Door

What Is There to Do on Campus?

Students can exercise, take a swim, or lift weights in the Life Sports Center. The college constantly has musical and theatrical performances in the Center for the Arts that are cheap or even free. Theater and music are really popular at Muhlenberg, so a lot of people turn out for those types of events. You can typically see a play or musical, band, dance show, or singing performance just about every weekend. Also, there are student bands, comedians, and karaoke in the Red Door. The Red Door also has free pool, air hockey, fooseball, and arcade games that you can play at any time. Free movies are shown in the Red Door on the big screen about once a month and can be really popular depending on the movie.

One thing college students learn to appreciate is the value of things that are free! Muhlenberg Activities Council does a really good job bringing in free entertainment for students, including everything from massages to stuff-a-plush. The events that draw the biggest crowds are the big name bands and comedians who come each year. Typically, concerts are held during the fall semester, and a comedian comes in the spring.

Movie Theater on Campus?

No, but free movies are often shown on the big screen in the Red Door on selected weekends.

Bowling on Campus?

No, but the Rose Bowl is a five-minute drive away.

Bar on Campus?

No, but Stooges is only a few blocks away. Some campus events are BYOB (bring your own beer).

Coffeehouse on Campus?

There is no actual coffeehouse on campus, but Java Joe's is a stand located by the fireplace and couches in Seegers Union. Java Joe's offers Starbucks coffee and specialty beverages in addition to baked goods.

Favorite Things to Do

On an average day, the most popular things to do on campus are probably hanging out in GQ, out on the lawn, and at the tables in Parents Plaza when it's nice out. When the nice weather hits, Frisbee golf is huge at Muhlenberg, and it's not uncommon to see people outside throwing Frisbees well past midnight.

Students Speak Out On...
Facilities

> "The facilities on campus are widely used, which helps bring the campus together. I enjoy going to the gym and lounging in the Red Door."

Q "For the most part, the facilities are great. Our student center, Seegers, is **very well kept and is a great place to hang out**. The computer labs are nice enough, and the library is beautiful."

Q "The facilities on campus are very nice. There is **a newly renovated fitness center**, and it looks great. The student union is nice; it has couches and a friendly environment."

Q "I love the way Moyer and Ettinger look as you walk down Academic Row, and the fact that even though I am Jewish, **walking into the chapel takes my breath away** just because it is so beautiful and welcoming!"

Q "Our facilities on campus are being upgraded to accommodate the increasing number of people on campus. They recently renovated the fitness center, and I hear that Seegers is the next place that will be expanded. **Seegers can get extremely crowded at high-traffic times** like lunch."

Q "One of the reasons that I was finally sold on coming here was how beautiful the campus is. On a nice day, I just look around and think how pretty everything is. Everything is always clean, and they are constantly repainting. **It's a very picturesque campus.**"

Q "Although the campus is small, **I never feel like we're lacking anything**. There are places to go to study and places to go to have fun. I feel like I have everything I need here, and it's all within a very short walk from my dorm."

Q "The facilities are **generally high quality**. The grounds are well kept, and the campus is very clean."

Q "I think the facilities are very nice. They are maintained very well, and the exteriors are appealing. They're always renovating to make buildings **more up-to-date, functional, and better looking**."

Q "My parents often joke that every time they visit Muhlenberg, we're having **something painted or renovated**. Muhlenberg really does a lot to keep our facilities looking great."

Q "Muhlenberg is a beautiful college, and so are its facilities. I'm really excited to see the renovated gym because it is supposed to be amazing. The student center is small, but then so is Muhlenberg. The bookstore has everything you need, and **I really like to study in the Red Door**; although, it would be nice if they served food down there, as well."

Q "Most of the facilities are very nice. The student union has **a cozy fireplace and student 'hangout' spot**."

Q "**I love the buildings on campus**. We have a great mix of the older more historical buildings like Haas and East along with the modern architecture of the CA and Moyer."

The College Prowler Take On...
Facilities

Seegers Union is the main facility on campus. It is rare for a student to go an entire day without entering Seegers as this is where the eateries, mailboxes, and bookstore are located in addition to several offices and the Red Door. Muhlenberg has a nice mixture of both traditional and modern buildings that makes your walk down Academic Row interesting. Egner Memorial Chapel is considered one of the finest modern Gothic campus chapels in the country, and it is the location of some of the most beautiful events on campus. The Baker Center for the Arts and Trexler Pavilion, on the other hand, are striking in how unique and modern their architecture is. Trexler Library is on the same side of the street as these buildings and is constructed in a similar style. While some libraries have the reputation of being dark and claustrophobic, Muhlenberg's library is actually quite bright and inviting. There are several study areas to the one side of the staircase as you walk down to the different levels; these areas have big comfy chairs and couches that are great for studying. In fact, they are so nice that it is not uncommon to spot a student napping in them.

Overall, Muhlenberg is a beautiful campus. Although the campus is small, there is plenty of open space for students to enjoy the outdoors. The walkways and fields are always clean and well kept, and the landscaping is attractive. In recent years, Muhlenberg has expanded to meet student needs with new dorms such as Robertson and South, and new academic buildings such as the innovative Moyer Hall. While building new facilities, Muhlenberg does everything it can to keep the older buildings well maintained. The facilities are always very clean, and they are constantly being repainted and refurbished to keep everything looking as good as new.

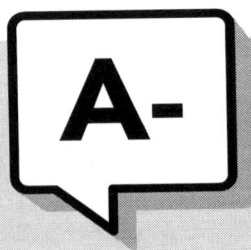

The College Prowler® Grade on
Facilities: A-

A high Facilities grade indicates that the campus is aesthetically pleasing and well-maintained; facilities are state-of-the-art, and libraries are exceptional. Other determining factors include the quality of both athletic and student centers and an abundance of things to do on campus.

Campus Dining

The Lowdown On...
Campus Dining

Freshman Meal Plan Requirement?
Yes

Meal Plan Average Cost:
$1,580

Places to Grab a Bite with Your Meal Plan:

Garden Room
Food: All-you-can-eat buffet, salad bar, home-style, pizza, sandwiches, desserts

Location: Seegers Union

Hours: Monday–Thursday 11 a.m.–7:30 p.m., Friday 11 a.m.–6:45 p.m., Saturday–Sunday 10:30 a.m.–6:45 p.m.

General's Quarters (GQ)

Food: Deli, grille, pizza, bakery, Action Station

Location: Seegers Union

Hours: Monday–Friday
7 a.m.–12 a.m., Saturday–Sunday 9 a.m.–6:45 p.m.,
7 p.m.–12 a.m.
Late Night (cash and flex dollars only): Friday–Saturday 12 a.m.–3 a.m.

Java Joe

Food: Coffee, sandwiches

Location: Kiosk in Seegers Union

Hours: Monday–Thursday
8:30 a.m.–8:30 p.m., Friday
8:30 a.m.–6 p.m.

Powerhouse Café

Food: Salads, sandwiches, desserts, Starbucks coffee

Location: Life Sports Center

Hours: Monday–Friday
8 a.m.–10 p.m., Saturday
11 a.m.–10 p.m.,
Sunday 1 p.m.–10 p.m.

Off-Campus Places to Use Your Meal Plan:

None

Did You Know?

Garden Room trays make excellent sleds! While GQ trays are easier to come by, the Garden Room trays are actually bigger and more slippery. Be nice, though, and return them when you're finished with your fun.

Muhlenberg students write comments and questions about the dining services and post them on the Napkin Board as you exit Garden Room. Every few days, the staff responds to these comments, and most of the time, they do their best to accommodate student requests.

Students Speak Out On...
Campus Dining

"Sometimes I get really sick of the food here, but then I kind of miss it when I go home! Pasta Day in GQ is my favorite."

Q "I really like GQ (General's Quarters) because it feels more like a café and less like a cafeteria. I do start to feel like I eat **the same food everyday**, but the Action Station has something different everyday of the week. I know a lot of people like Garden Room because it has a really large variety of food, and Java Joe's has awesome coffee and really good cookies."

Q "The food here is pretty decent; **it just gets repetitive**. When you think about it, though, your food at home can get repetitive too! So, I don't mind this too much. My friends and I like to switch it up by rotating between Garden Room and GQ."

Q "The food on campus is **better than a lot of other colleges** I visited in high school. I have a fairly restricted diet, but I can always make something that works for me in the Garden Room. I enjoy getting coffee at Java Joe's; maybe a little too much!"

Q "The food is delicious, but we tend to get our favorites over and over, so it can become repetitive. I prefer the Garden Room because of the **variety, speed, and cost**. If you purchase five cents over a swipe in GQ, you must pay by cash or swipe again."

Q "For the most part, I am satisfied with the food here. There is **usually a good variety in the Garden Room**, and the GQ is good for a quick lunch or snacks. I really like the Action Stations because they cater to students' preferences, and they are willing to listen to feedback and make changes if there are complaints."

Q "I really like the food on campus, especially the **mozzarella sticks and chicken parmesan**. I love the 'hi-tech' atmosphere of the General's Quarters."

Q "Nothing compares to a home-cooked meal, but bagel bombs at GQ are **the best breakfast food** and late-night snack!"

Q "The food is good for college food, but **you get sick of eating the same things** over and over and over again."

Q "The food, **while not home-cooked, is actually very good**. I've had friends from other colleges come to visit and comment on the quality of our food. One of my favorite things about the dining hall is that they have a 'Napkin Board.' Students write down likes/dislikes/comments/compliments on a napkin and stick it to the board. Every so often, the staff will write up a response, and hopefully, accommodate your request."

Q "Although the food isn't bad, it can definitely get redundant because **GQ almost always has the same options**, and Garden Room has a weekly schedule that is repeated throughout the semester."

The College Prowler Take On...
Campus Dining

For many people, it could be easy to gain the Freshman 15 at Muhlenberg because the food is generally decent. The meal plans work on a "swipe system;" depending on the level of your meal plan, you have a different number of swipes per week or semester. These swipes can be used in Garden Room or General's Quarters (GQ). Garden Room is more like a cafeteria, and it is all-you-can-eat for one swipe. Garden Room is good when you want to eat a lot or have a healthier eating habit. The frozen yogurt machines are also a staple of Garden Room, and you will often hear people commenting on the "fro yo quality" because after going to Muhlenberg for a semester, you will develop a type of frozen yogurt elite ranking that only Muhlenberg pros understand. One note of caution: it seems that by the end of the week, the chefs take a break and the pickings get very slim.

With the exception of the great Saturday brunch, most people stick to GQ on the weekends. GQ is where you find more of the fast food type of meals. One swipe is worth $4.10, and you have to swipe again, or pay with cash or debit, if you want more than that. Tuesdays and Fridays are "Pasta Day" in GQ, and this is probably the most popular food on campus. The lines go out the door during the busiest lunch hours, but it is well worth the wait if you have the time. If you eat there enough, a lot of the staff gets to know you, and does not even need to ask how you want your pasta.

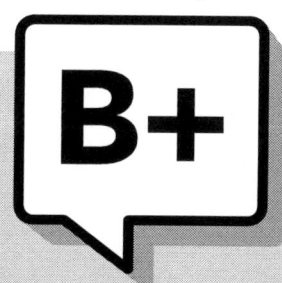

The College Prowler® Grade on Campus Dining: B+

Our grade on Campus Dining addresses the quality of both school-owned dining halls and independent on-campus restaurants as well as the price, availability, and variety of food.

Off-Campus Dining

The Lowdown On...
Off-Campus Dining

Restaurant Prowler: Popular Places to Eat!

Applebee's
Food: American
1510 Cedar Crest Blvd.
(610) 530-2450
Cool Features: Half price appetizers after 9 p.m. Sunday–Thursday.
Price: $8–$15 per person
Hours: Monday–Thursday 11 a.m.–11 p.m., Friday–Sunday 11 a.m.–2 a.m.

Attilio's Restaurant & Pizzeria
Food: Italian, hoagies, pizza
1500 N Cedar Crest Blvd.
(610) 395-7006
Price: $8–$15 per person
Hours: Sunday–Thursday 11 a.m.–9:30 p.m., Friday–Saturday 11 a.m.–10 p.m.

Bay Leaf Restaurant
Food: American, Asian
935 Hamilton St.
(610) 433-4211
www.allentownbayleaf.com

(Bay Leaf Restaurant, continued)

Price: $15–$20 per person

Hours: Monday–Friday 11:30 a.m.–2 p.m., 5 p.m.–10 p.m., Saturday 5 p.m.–10 p.m.

Bennigan's Grill and Tavern

Food: American, Irish

2835 Lehigh St.

(610) 791-7900

www.bennigans.com

Price: $10–$20 per person

Hours: Sunday–Thursday 11 a.m.–10 p.m., Friday–Saturday 11 a.m.–12 a.m.

Bethlehem Brew Works

Food: American

569 Main St., Bethlehem

(610) 882-1300

www.thebrewworks.com

Cool Features: Beer brewed on site

Price: $10–$20 per person

Hours: Sunday–Wednesday 11 a.m.–11 p.m., Thursday–Saturday 11 a.m.–12 a.m., Bar open daily until 2 a.m.

Bucca di Beppo

Food: Italian

714 Grape St.

(610) 264-4268

www.bucadibeppo.com

(Buca di Beppo, continued)

Price: $10–$20 per person

Hours: Monday–Thursday 5 p.m.–10 p.m., Friday 5 p.m.–11 p.m., Saturday 12 p.m.–11 p.m., Sunday 12 p.m.–9 p.m.

Carmine's Restaurant

Food: Italian

1052 Union Blvd.

(610) 433-7711

Cool Features: Weekend entertainment, BYOB.

Price: $10–$20 per person

Hours: Monday–Thursday 11 a.m.–9 p.m., Friday–Saturday 11 a.m.–10 p.m., Sunday 3 p.m.–9 p.m.

Carrabas Italian Grill

Food: Italian

Cedar Crest & Hamilton Blvds.

(610) 439-6100

www.carrabas.com

Cool Features: Great bread.

Price: $10–$20 per person

Hours: Monday–Thursday 4 p.m.–10 p.m., Friday–Saturday 4 p.m.–11 p.m., Saturday 3 p.m.–11 p.m., Sunday 12 p.m.–9:30 p.m.

Charlie Brown's Steakhouse

Food: Seafood, steak, chicken

1908 Walbert Ave.

(610) 437-1070

www.charliebrowns.com

(Charlie Brown's Steakhouse, continued)

Cool Features: Bar, lounge, nightly specials, happy hour.

Price: $10–$20 per person

Hours: Monday–Thursday 11;30 a.m.–2:30 p.m., 3 p.m.–10 p.m., Friday–Saturday 11:30 a.m.–2:30 p.m., 3 p.m.–10:30 p.m., Sunday 11:30 a.m.–9 p.m.

Chili's

Food: American, Southwest

815 Grape St., Whitehall

(610) 264-4400

Price: $8–$15 per person

Hours: Sunday–Thursday 11 a.m.–10 p.m., Friday–Saturday 11 a.m.–12 a.m.

Don Pablo's

Food: Mexican

2610 MacArthur Rd., Whitehall

(610) 435-4424

www.donpablos.com

Price: $8–$15 per person

Hours: Sunday–Thursday 11 a.m.–10 p.m., Friday–Saturday 11:30 a.m.–11 p.m.

Friendly's

Food: American

Cedar Crest & Hamilton Blvds.

(610) 770-9883

www.friendlys.com

Price: $8–$15 per person

Hours: Sunday–Thursday 7 a.m.–11 p.m., Friday–Saturday 7 a.m.–12 a.m.

Hunan Springs

4939 Hamilton Blvd., Wecosville

(610) 366-8338

Price: $5–$10 per person

Hours: Monday–Saturday 11:30 a.m.–10 p.m., Sunday 11:30 a.m.–9 p.m.

King George Inn

Food: Continental

Cedar Crest & Hamilton Blvds.

(610) 435-1723

Cool Features: Outdoor dining, national historic site built in 1756.

Price: $10–$25 per person

Hours: Monday–Thursday 11:30 a.m.–4 p.m., 4 p.m.–10 p.m., Friday–Saturday 11:30 a.m.–4 p.m., 4 p.m.–11:30 p.m., Sunday 4 p.m.–10 p.m.

Lehigh Valley Diner

1162 MacArthur Rd., Whitehall

(610) 434-8886

Price: $5–$10 per person

Hours: Daily 24 hours

LoBaido's Café & Gelateria

Food: Italian

442 N 8th St.

(610) 820-7570

Cool Features: Homemade ice cream.

Price: $5–$20 per person

Hours: Daily 11 a.m.–10 p.m.

Louie's Restaurant

Food: Italian

1207 Chew St.

(610) 434-2340

Cool Features: BYOB.

www.louiesrestaurant.com

Price: $10–$20 per person

Hours: Monday–Friday
11 a.m.–10 p.m., Saturday
4 p.m.–10 p.m., Sunday
4 p.m.–9 p.m.

Mario's Pizza Café

Food: Pizza, American, Italian

3245 Hamilton Blvd.

(610) 435-4484

Price: $5–$10 per person

Hours: Sunday–Thursday
10 a.m.–10 p.m., Friday–Saturday 10 a.m.–11 p.m.

Olive Garden

Food: Italian

715 Grape St., Whitehall

(610) 266-6777

www.olivegarden.com

Price: $10–$20 per person

Hours: Sunday–Thursday
11 a.m.–10 p.m., Friday–Saturday 11 a.m.–11 p.m.

Outback Steakhouse

Food: American

3100 W Tilghman St.

(610) 437-7117

Price: $10–$20 per person

(Outback Steakhouse, continued)

Hours: Monday–Thursday
4 p.m.–10:30 p.m., Friday
4 p.m.–11 p.m., Saturday
2 p.m.–11 p.m., Sunday
2 p.m.–9:30 p.m.

Perkins

Food: American, bakery

Cedar Crest & Hamilton Blvds.

(610) 820-5767

www.perkinsrestaurants.com

Price: $8–$15 per person

Hours: Daily 6 a.m.–12 a.m..

Pistachio's Bar and Grill

Food: Italian, Mediterranean

341 S Cedar Crest Blvd.

(610) 435-7007

www.pistachiobarandgrille.com

Cool Features: Bar, heated, outdoor café.

Price: $15–$20 per person

Hours: Sunday–Thursday
11:30 a.m.–12 a.m., Friday–Saturday 11:30 a.m.–2 a.m., Sunday 11:30 a.m.–3 p.m.

Red Lobster

Food: Seafood

800 Lehigh Valley Mall, Whitehall

(610) 264-5541

Price: $15–$20 per person

Hours: Sunday–Thursday
10 a.m.–10 p.m., Friday–Saturday 10 a.m.–11 p.m.

Red Robin
Food: American
Tilghman Square
(610) 366-1776
Cool Features: Bottomless french fries, gourmet burgers.
Price: $10–$15 per person
Hours: Monday–Saturday 11 a.m.–12 a.m., Sunday 11 a.m.–11 p.m.

Rookie's Restaurant & Sports Pub
1328 W Tilghman St.
(610) 821-8484
Price: $10–$15 per person
Hours: Daily 11:30 a.m.–2 a.m.

The Shanty
Food: Seafood, steak, chicken
617 N 19th St.
(610) 437-5358
Cool Features: Live entertainment.
Price: $10–$20 per person
Hours: Monday–Thursday 11:30 a.m.–9 p.m., Friday–Saturday 11:30 a.m.–10 p.m., Sunday 11 a.m.–3 p.m., 4 p.m.–8 p.m.

Stooges
2105 W Liberty St.
(610) 432-7553
www.stoogesbarandgrille.com
Cool Features: Live music on Sunday and Thursday.

(Stooges, continued)
Price: $8–$15 per person
Hours: Wednesday–Saturday 11 a.m.–12 a.m., Sunday–Tuesday 11 a.m.–11 p.m.

T.G.I.Friday's
Food: American
395 S Cedar Crest Blvd.
(610) 776-8188
www.tgifridays.com
Cool Features: Happy hour, trivia games.
Price: $10–$12 per person
Hours: Sunday–Thursday 11 a.m.–12 a.m., Friday–Saturday 11 a.m.–2 a.m.

Yocco's Hot Dog King
625 W Liberty St.
(610) 433-1950
Cool Features: An Allentown tradition since 1922. Try their "secret recipe" chili sauce.
Price: $1–$5 per person
Hours: Sunday–Thursday 10:30 a.m.–10 p.m., Friday–Saturday 10:30 a.m.–11 p.m.

Other Places to Check Out:
Chicken Lounge
China King
Fusion Grill
McDonald's
Panera Bread
Papa John's
Wendy's

Student Favorites:
Bucca di Beppo
Carrabas Italian Grill
Louie's Restaurant
The Shanty

Late-Night Dining:
Applebee's
T.G.I.Friday's

24-Hour Eating:
Wegman's
Lehigh Valley Diner

Closest Grocery Stores:
Giant
3100 W Tilghman St.
Allentown
(610) 351-2091

King's Market
365 S Cedar Crest Blvd.
Allentown
(610) 821-4550

(Closest Grocery Stores, continued)
Wegman's
3900 Tilghman St.
Allentown
(610) 336-7900

Best Pizza:
Mario's Pizza Café

Best Chinese:
Hunan Springs

Best Breakfast:
Perkins

Best Wings:
Rookie's Restaurant & Sports Pub
Stooges

Best Place to Take Your Parents:
The Shanty
Louie's Restaurant
Bucca di Beppo

Students Speak Out On...
Off-Campus Dining

"There are quite a few restaurants within a five-minute drive from campus. They range from your burger joint to fine and classy; it's very nice."

Q "There are some good restaurants off campus that students can go to together or with their families when they come to visit. **T.G.I.Friday's is a popular place**, and there's also Friendly's, Perkins, and Carrabas. The Muhlenberg Shuttle goes to them, so you're not stranded if you don't have a car."

Q "When you get tired of Garden Room and GQ, eating off campus is a great change of pace. There are so **many restaurants nearby** that you can go somewhere different each time if you look around."

Q "There are many restaurants off campus, and they come in all shapes and sizes. **It's fun to bring friends along** and find them all."

Q "If I had more money, **I'd eat out every weekend**. There are so many good places to eat around campus."

Q "I love Pistachio's and Carrabas! They both have **excellent food and great atmospheres**. Panera Bread and Mario's Pizza Café are also good places to eat."

Q "There are **a lot of good restaurants off campus**. A lot of people also like to order from China King or Papa John's."

Q "Chili's has the best appetizers. **Try the sampler!**"

Q "We have a really wide variety of restaurants near campus. They range from McDonald's and Wendy's, to Outback Steakhouse and T.G.I.Friday's, and then there are **fancy places like the Fusion Grill and Carrabas**."

Q "The Lehigh Valley is known for having excellent places to eat. **You have your typical good chains**, but then there are some other really excellent places like the Shanty, Charlie Brown's, Bethlehem Brew Works, and King George Inn."

Q "If you're willing to venture downtown, **you can have a lot of fun finding the more unique restaurants** that offer a great change from the typical chains."

Q "It may sound weird because it's a grocery store, but you can actually have **a really good time getting dinner** at Wegman's with your friends. You can do your shopping at the same time, too!"

Q "The restaurants nearby are good. There are tons of your typical chain restaurants, and there are some other good finds, too. **I suggest the Chicken Lounge** for drinks and nachos."

The College Prowler Take On...
Off-Campus Dining

There are many restaurants that are within a short distance from campus. You can find everything from your cheap fast food at McDonald's to fine dining at King George Inn. Being able to explore all of the restaurants in the area is definitely a benefit of having a car on campus. Don't worry though—the Muhlenberg Shuttle will take you to most of the big restaurants near campus, and you could even walk to a few of them if you were desperate. Bucca di Beppo and the Shanty are two popular places that are on the more expensive side, but it's typically agreed that they're well worth the money. All of the big chain restaurants are easy to find, and Allentown also has a great variety of smaller, privately-owned restaurants. Most of these places, such as LoBaido's, are located downtown and require a little more searching.

As far as restaurants go, there isn't much that Allentown doesn't offer. Although the food on campus isn't bad, it can lack variety. For this reason, eating out is one of the things that students enjoy doing off campus the most. It's great to be able to get off campus for something other than the usual Garden Room or GQ selections. Most students would eat out more if they had more time and money. Luckily, there are restaurants that are close and inexpensive. Yet, there are also a number of restaurants available for special occasions or when the family comes to visit.

The College Prowler® Grade on
Off-Campus Dining: C+

A high Off-Campus Dining grade implies that off-campus restaurants are affordable, accessible, and worth visiting. Other factors include the variety of cuisine and the availability of alternative options (vegetarian, vegan, Kosher, etc.).

Campus Housing

The Lowdown On...
Campus Housing

Room Types:
Singles
Doubles
Triples
Quads

Best Dorms:
Robertson Hall
South Hall
Taylor Hall
Walz Hall

Worst Dorms:
East Halls
Prosser Hall

Undergrads Living on Campus:
91%

Number of Dormitories:
9

Number of University-Owned Apartments:
50+ units

Dormitories:

Benfer Hall — 8 people
Floors: 3
Total Occupancy: 114
Bathrooms: Shared by suite
Coed: By suite
Residents: Upperclassmen
Room Types: Suites with four doubles
Special Features: Central air-conditioning, computer lab, laundry, private entrance, and living room for each suite.

Brown Hall
Floors: 4
Total Occupancy: 180
Bathrooms: Shared by floor
Coed: No, all female
Residents: Freshmen and upperclassmen
Room Types: Singles, doubles, triples, quads
Special Features: High ceilings, big windows, two study lounges, computer labs, kitchen, TV lounge, laundry.

East Halls — worst.
Floors: 7 three-story sections
Total Occupancy: 176
Bathrooms: Shared by floor
Coed: By wing/floor
Residents: Upperclassmen
Room Types: Singles, doubles, triples
Special Features: Computer lab, laundry, study lounge, access to the Martin Luther Underground.

Martin Luther Hall
Floors: 4
Total Occupancy: 240
Bathrooms: Shared by floor
Coed: By floor
Residents: Upperclassmen
Room Types: Singles, doubles, triples
Special Features: Computer labs, study lounge, laundry, Martin Luther Underground with kitchen, game room, and TV lounge.

Prosser Hall
Floors: 3
Total Occupancy: 270
Bathrooms: Shared by floor or wing
Coed: By floor
Residents: Freshmen
Room Types: Singles, doubles, quads
Special Features: Game room, kitchen, laundry, study lounges, computer labs, Campus Safety and Residential Services are housed in the basement.

Robertson Hall
Floors: 4
Total Occupancy: 68
Bathrooms: Shared by suite; toilet room, shower room, two-sink vanity
Coed: By suite
Residents: Upperclassmen
Room Types: Suites with four singles
Special Features: Central air-conditioning, laundry, kitchens, living room, rec rooms.

South Hall
Floors: 4
Total Occupancy: 72
Bathrooms: Shared by suite; toilet room, shower room, two-sink vanity
Coed: By suite
Residents: Upperclassmen
Room Types: Suites with four singles
Special Features: Central air-conditioning, laundry, kitchens, living room, rec rooms.

Taylor Hall
Floors: 4
Total Occupancy: 113
Bathrooms: In-room
Coed: By room
Residents: Upperclassmen
Room Types: Prime doubles
Special Features: Air-conditioning, private bathrooms, computer labs, study lounges, TV lounge

Walz Hall
Floors: 4
Total Occupancy: 190
Bathrooms: Shared by floor
Coed: By wing/room
Residents: Freshmen
Room Types: Singles, doubles, triples
Special Features: Central air-conditioning, laundry, game room, kitchen, TV lounge, computer lab.

Apartments:

MacGregor Village
Total Occupancy: 56
Bathrooms: Private
Coed: By apartment
Residents: Upperclassmen
Room Types: 2-bedroom apartments, each housing four students
Special Features: Central air-conditioning, full private kitchen, laundry, computer lab.

MILE (Muhlenberg Independent Living Experience) Housing
MILE housing is Muhlenberg-owned off-campus housing. 2-, 3-, 4-person houses, as well as leased properties, are available.

See *www.muhlenberg.edu/mgt/resserv/milelotterydescriptionlist.html* for details

Housing Offered:
Singles: 10%
Doubles: 68%
Triplet/Suites: 5%
Apartments: 17%

Available for Rent
Micro fridge with refrigerator, freezer, microwave

Bed Type
Twin (some extra-long), some bunk beds, some lofts

What You Get
Bed, desk and chair, dresser, closet or wardrobe, free campus and local telephone calls, personal Internet and telephone lines, optional cable, window shades

Cleaning Service?
In public areas. Community bathrooms are cleaned by staff daily.

Also Available
Special-interest housing is available to students who go through the special-interest application process.

Room Descriptions
Residence Rooms include standard, prime, and suite-style units.

Standard – Students share a large, central bathroom facility (most first-year students are assigned to these rooms).

Prime – Students share a private or semi-private bathroom with no more than five students.

Suite-style – Students share a semi-private bathroom and a common living area.

Apartments – The apartments on campus are owned by the college, and consist of units for four students with two doubles, a bathroom, a common area, and full kitchen.

Did You Know?

East is Muhlenberg's oldest residence hall, built way back in 1903.

All of Muhlenberg's dorms are smoke-free facilities.

Muhlenberg guaruntees that a student will have housing for **all four years**.

Students Speak Out On...
Campus Housing

> "I lived in Prosser as a freshman. Everyone always says to avoid living there, but I had a great time because it's really social."

Q "As a freshman, you are limited to three dorms. Walz is the nicest of these dorms, as it has air-conditioning and slightly larger rooms. Brown is just for girls, and it houses upperclassmen, as well. I was heartbroken when I was told that I would be living in Brown. In the end, though, it worked out well. The rooms are very large for the most part, and **there are no rules about having guys in your room**."

Q "I think Muhlenberg's dorms are very nice. I can't complain about any of my experiences so far. **Prosser is the 'party dorm' for freshmen**. It houses the most freshmen, and is often referred to as the 'ghetto dorm.' Walz is the newest of the freshman dorms, and it is air conditioned. Most students living there usually get into Muhlenberg early decision, and therefore have first dibs on ranking which dorm they want to live in."

Q "Every dorm is different, and some are better than others. Brown is great if you don't mind being with all girls because it has high ceilings and a lot of space. As far as freshman dorms go, Walz is nicer and air conditioned, but Prosser is definitely more social. **Taylor is really nice for upperclassmen** because you only share a bathroom with your roommate. No more shower shoes!"

Q "The dorms are actually quite nice. **They aren't very big**, so they give the feeling of a close community."

Q "Brown is really nice as a freshman, except that only girls can live there. **It can be nice and cozy at times**, but you also tend to feel like you are out of the loop a little bit by living there. I think Walz is ideal for freshmen, and Taylor or the new suites are really nice for after that."

Q "I have lived in Prosser, Brown, Walz, Martin Luther, and East, so I have had my fair share of housing experiences. I think that **each dorm has both good and bad points**. I really liked living in the Prosser Annex freshman year. Our whole floor became really close; yet, Main Prosser was right out the door if we wanted to see what was going on in the main hall."

Q "Overall, the dorms are in excellent condition. In Taylor, each double is equipped with **air-conditioning and a bathroom**. South and Robertson have a galley kitchen, living room, four bedrooms, and a bathroom. Even the older buildings, such as Brown and East, are pretty nice for the most part. In Brown and East, each room is different, giving them character. East does have a bug problem."

Q "I loved living in Prosser my freshman year; I wouldn't trade the experience I had there. I am **still friends with the people who lived on my floor**!"

Q "The dorms are mostly nice. As a freshman, **definitely try to get into Walz**. There is air-conditioning, big rooms, and it is just very nice."

Q "I think you can manage to be happy in any dorm Muhlenberg has to offer. There are positive and negative things about each when you get right down to it. Even though it's a small campus, it makes things feel so much cozier when **you can just wander to your friend's room at all hours**."

The College Prowler Take On...
Campus Housing

As a freshman, you have three options: Prosser, Walz, and Brown. Brown is the all-girls dorm with high ceilings and huge windows. If you don't mind the quiet atmosphere and lack of guys, you should probably try for Brown. Walz is typically the most desired of the dorms, and is actually even nicer than a lot of the options for upperclassmen. It is the newest of the freshmen dorms, has the biggest rooms, and is the only one that is air conditioned. Do not be overly distressed if you end up in Prosser; you will be in good company since it is the largest of the dorms on campus. Sure, you share your bathroom with the most people, and it is constantly loud in the hallways, but you will never feel lonely and are sure to meet a lot of people while standing outside during the inevitable fire alarms set off by someone's burnt popcorn.

Housing freshman year is supposedly based on how soon you turn in your deposit with your housing preferences. For this reason, a large portion of Walz is made up of students who applied early decision. Although some people are upset if they aren't placed in their first choice, most people are able to make the best of their situation because there are benefits to each of the dorms. Some are newer and bigger than others, but there are very few rooms in any of the dorms on campus that are unbearable. Everyone is eager to meet people during this first year, so you will be able to make friends anywhere you live. After freshman year, you enter the lottery system, which is perhaps the most dramatic time of year on campus. It suddenly seems that your friendships and happiness for the entire next year come down to depending on one number that you receive in your mailbox at random. Housing after freshman year at Muhlenberg is varied and really depends on your luck in the lottery. During housing, remember to do as much research as you can before choosing a room and to try to stay friends with those who have better numbers.

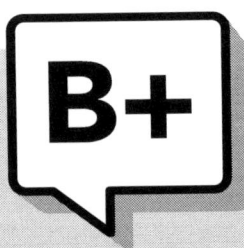

The College Prowler® Grade on
Campus Housing: B+

A high Campus Housing grade indicates that dorms are clean, well-maintained, and spacious. Other determining factors include variety of dorms, proximity to classes, and social atmosphere.

Off-Campus Housing

The Lowdown On...
Off-Campus Housing

Undergrads in Off-Campus Housing:
9%

Average Rent for:
Studio Apt.: $450/month
1-BR Apt.: $600/month
2-BR Apt.: $750/month

Best Time to Look for a Place:
Beginning of the spring semester

Popular Areas

The Tremont Apartments are now becoming popular areas for students to live because they are off campus, and now they are part of the MILE (Muhlenberg Independent Living Experience) property lottery. In Tremont Apartments, there are 15 units available for two people and 13 units available for three people. Although Tremont Apartments are furnished in the same way as the MILE properties, they do not come with all of the same services as MILE properties, such as a campus phone number. MILE properties fall somewhere between on-campus and off-campus housing. To live in a MILE property, you need to fill out an off-campus housing application. However, some of the properties are so close that you are practically on campus. For students looking for housing totally separate from the college, the area around 17th Street is popular.

Students Speak Out On...
Off-Campus Housing

"**Personally, I don't think off-campus housing is very convenient.** For example, the Tremont Apartments are six blocks off campus, so its residents tend to become pretty isolated."

Q "**I don't really see off-campus housing being worth it.** I like being close to all the buildings and stuff."

Q "I decided to **stay on campus all four years**. I just like the idea of waking up 10 minutes before class and still making it there in time!"

Q "Living **on campus makes life easier** because you are always near your home."

Q "I prefer to live on campus. **Very few students move off campus until junior or senior year**. Even then, the large majority live in housing that is affiliated with the college. It's nice being on campus and having everything at your fingertips."

Q "After living on campus for the first two years, a lot of people enjoy **the freedom of living off campus** later. The school owns a decent number of MILE houses, and many people choose to do that. I also have a bunch of friends living off campus through Allentown Realty. It is worth it to live off campus, as nothing is that far away from school."

Q "I know a couple of people who do live off campus, and **they seem satisfied**. I would imagine, though, that it would be pretty inconvenient."

Q "I would love to live in a MILE house. It is the perfect compromise as far as I'm concerned. **You can have the freedom and space of having your own place**, but the school still takes care of you. There's less to worry about than living in an apartment somewhere in Allentown."

Q "**I like living on campus** because I need my quick naps when I have a break from class."

Q "Living off campus can be nice because you have more space, and it's easier to make your own food. **When I say off campus, I really mean MILE houses**. I wouldn't want to go through the hassle of living somewhere that wasn't owned by Muhlenberg."

Q "Some of the MILE houses are really nice, but there's always a risk that you'll end up in **one that isn't desirable**. I've never even considered living completely off campus; I love being able to walk to class in less than 10 minutes."

Q "The school does everything it can to keep you from living in housing that isn't owned by them. The school doesn't help you at all, and **it is highly discouraged**."

Q "If you're involved in a lot of things on campus, **it's so much easier to live there**."

The College Prowler Take On...
Off-Campus Housing

Living off campus can be a great way to really enjoy the independence that comes with college life, and while this way of life is very appealing to some students, it is not for everyone. There are also disadvantages to getting out of the residence halls; with more independence also comes more responsibility. Also, Muhlenberg doesn't make independent living convenient for its students. To live off campus, students are required to fill out an application and meet certain requirements; they must be in good academic standing with a GPA of at least 2.5 and attend a meeting during the spring semester. Even after doing this, authorization to live off campus is not guaranteed. Until students receive a letter of approval in the mail, they're not permitted to sign a lease. Also, students are ineligible for future housing lotteries after going off campus.

Many Muhlenberg students choose to pick the option that falls right in the middle of dorms and off-campus housing. Muhlenberg Independent Living Experience (MILE) properties are Muhlenberg-owned, off-campus apartments and houses for students. The popular Tremont Apartments, part of MILE housing, are about a five-minute drive from campus. Students wishing to live in MILE houses or Tremont must also go through an application process, but it is not as difficult as the off-campus procedure. There are MILE places that are really beautiful and others that are not quite as desirable. Ultimately, living off campus is a matter of personal preference. Some students miss the luxury of being able to roll out of bed and make it to class in five minutes, and others love having more space and no RA.

The College Prowler® Grade on Off-Campus Housing: C+

A high grade in Off-Campus Housing indicates that apartments are of high quality, close to campus, affordable, and easy to secure.

Diversity

The Lowdown On...
Diversity

Native American:
Less than 1%

Asian American:
2%

African American:
2%

Hispanic:
4%

White:
91%

International:
Less than 1%

Unknown:
1%

Out-of-State:
69%

Political Activity

If you're interested in politics, there are plenty of opportunities to participate in political activities on campus. Several organizations sponsor letter writing campaigns, and there is a group that promotes voting registration. The College Republicans and College Democrats are fairly visible on campus, and they host a variety of speakers, trips, and discussions throughout the semester.

Gay Pride

Muhlenberg is very accepting of gay students on campus. Gay Straight Alliance (GSA) sponsors several events throughout the year to promote acceptance and tolerance. Besides these structured events, the campus is just really accepting in general. While the exact number of homosexual students may not be known, it's not something that is hidden on campus.

Most Popular Religions

Muhlenberg has quite a few religious student organizations. There are several different Christian groups in addition to Hillel. With over two-thirds of Jewish students as members of Hillel, it is the largest student organization on campus.

Economic Status

The majority of students come from middle- to upper-class economic backgrounds. While there are a lot of students who are from typical middle class families, it is not uncommon to notice the new BMW in the parking lot either.

Minority Clubs

There are several minority clubs at Muhlenberg, but they aren't among the most visible organizations on campus. Muhlenberg does what it can to promote acceptance and learning about different cultures; these groups just aren't the most advertised and have fewer members than a lot of other clubs.

Students Speak Out On...
Diversity

> "Although the campus itself is not very diverse, there are a lot of events on campus to promote diversity awareness."

Q "In terms of ethnicity and race, the campus is not very diverse. The campus is diverse, however, when looking at the types of people. I mean, when you realize that our top two majors are probably theater and pre-med, you can imagine how different the students are. There are also **a lot of religious differences**. We may be a Lutheran college, but that doesn't seem to deter people from other religions."

Q "Muhlenberg is not very diverse at all. The overwhelming majority of students are white, and **most come from middle- to upper-class families**. As far as religion, it's a bit more diverse. Although Muhlenberg is Lutheran affiliated, I think about one-third of students are Jewish."

Q "Muhlenberg is very diverse from person to person, if we are talking about personalities. That's an important thing to remember, because people think the campus is not diverse just because it is **not very racially or geographically diverse**."

Q "Religiously, the campus is very diverse. Ethnically, it's not quite as diverse. It's mostly made up of **white, suburban, tri-state kids**."

Q "**The campus is not very diverse**; it's one of my main concerns about the college."

Q "Muhlenberg is **very diverse in terms of interests and ideas**, but not at all in terms of location and race."

Q "Religiously, the campus is very diverse. Racially, we are probably **one of the least diverse colleges in the nation**. The college is trying really hard to work on the diversity of our students."

Q "Our school is definitely **more religiously and culturally diverse than racially** diverse."

Q "I come from a town where I didn't know one Jewish person growing up. Muhlenberg has exposed me to **a lot of people who are different religions** and have different beliefs. If you mean racially, though, we aren't very diverse in that way."

Q "**I've learned about a lot of different cultures in college**, but not because of the racial diversity on campus. We don't have that much, but I have learned things in class."

Q "Compared to my high school, Muhlenberg is definitely lacking in diversity. I think **it's important to realize that there are students who are minorities**, and they don't seem to have any problems. It's not like Muhlenberg isn't accepting of people; if anything, I think Muhlenberg is more accepting of all people than my high school ever was."

The College Prowler Take On...
Diversity

Diversity is not something for which Muhlenberg is well known. This isn't to say that minorities are not present on campus, but racial diversity is definitely lacking. The large majority of Muhlenberg students are white from the same general geographic and economic background. But when you look at diversity as being broader than just these areas, that's when Muhlenberg has more to offer. Religiously, Muhlenberg is much more diverse than many of the towns and high schools students come from. The student population is also diverse when considering the types of people and eclectic variety of majors. Some students come here for the great pre-med program, and some come because they have heard about Muhlenberg's excellent reputation for theater. Just because a lot of people here may be of the same race, it doesn't mean that they don't have different lifestyles that you can learn about.

While the 'Berg may not have a large representation of racial minorities on campus, other types of diversity are present. There are a variety of religions and sexual orientations. Although the student population may be homogeneous racially, there are still many opportunities to learn about different cultures. Muhlenberg puts a lot of effort in teaching students about different cultures and stresses acceptance of all types of people.

The College Prowler® Grade on
Diversity: D-

A high grade in Diversity indicates that ethnic minorities and international students have a notable presence on campus and that students of different economic backgrounds, religious beliefs, and sexual preferences are well-represented.

Guys & Girls

The Lowdown On...
Guys & Girls

Men Undergrads:
41%

Women Undergrads:
59%

Social Scene

In general, Muhlenberg is a very social and friendly campus. There are obviously some people who are shy or not as outgoing as others, but most people go out of their way to act friendly. When you walk down Academic Row, most people will say hello even if they don't know you. Sure, there are some cliques on campus, but there isn't too much of a social hierarchy. Most people are pretty accepting and willing to hang out with different types of people.

Hookups or Relationships?

It seems like most relationships start out as being casual since you can just hang out in the dorms with different people. You don't usually need to make specific plans to go out on dates. Most students end up hooking up with people who live on their floor or are already in their group of friends. After relationships start, though, they seem to get serious pretty quickly, partially because the campus is so small. It's very easy to spend the majority of your time with the person you are dating, and you inevitably end up running into the person all over campus. After saying this, random hookups are possible if that's what you're looking for. Even though there are a lot of serious relationships, there are also a lot of commitment-free hookups that occur. You just have to keep in mind that Muhlenberg isn't a huge university where you can safely avoid seeing the person around campus come Monday.

Best Place to Meet Guys/Girls

Since so much of your time is spent in the classrooms, or in the dorms, these are probably the most common places to meet a significant other. The dorms are really good for this because it's such a relaxed atmosphere. It's not like when you're in high school and you need to make plans to go over to someone's house to see them. In dorms, you just walk over to someone's room any time you want to hang out, or just to say hi. This is especially true in freshman dorms because a lot of people leave their doors open and are eager to meet new people. Joining clubs can be a good way to meet people with similar interests. You can also meet people just by hanging out in Seegers, or on the lawn, when it's nice out.

If you're looking to meet people in less of a "school" atmosphere, hit the frat or house parties on the weekends. Tired of Muhlenberg students? There are also clubs and bars nearby that a lot of college students go to at night. Remember that there are several other colleges such as Lehigh that are within a short driving distance.

Dress Code

For the most part, people tend to dress preppy here. In certain classes, there will be a few people who just roll out of bed and come to class in sweats; however, it is just as common to see a few girls in heels and guys in dress shirts. There are some eclectic dressers and some go with the skater look or something else that is a little bit more unique. These people, however, are out-numbered by those who wear the more typical attire that would probably be classified as preppy casual.

Did You Know?

Top Three Places to Find Hotties:
1. Fraternities
2. Gym
3. Seegers Union

Top Places to Hook Up:
1. Fraternities
2. House parties
3. Dorms
4. Victor's Lament
5. 50-yard line

Students Speak Out On...
Guys & Girls

> "You don't really find the 'tough guy' jocks here, and the girls are sweet and hot! Students are admitted to Muhlenberg because they have a fun personality."

Q "I think that Muhlenberg is **a good-looking school**. Many people get dressed up and made up for class. It is not unheard of for girls to wear heels and straighten their hair regularly. People are obviously concerned about their looks. In my opinion, it can be a bit much. Not everyone is this superficial, though."

Q "I think people at Muhlenberg are pretty nice for the most part. Sometimes, students can be a bit spoiled and interested in status, but not everyone is like that. Plus, I think most people are willing to help you out if you ever need them. As far as being hot, **there are some hot people**. I think that's all in the eye of the beholder, though."

Q "Muhlenberg is **a very beautiful campus** as far as people are concerned."

Q "When I first came here, I was amazed at how much better looking and well dressed the people here were than in my high school. **The majority of the school dresses preppy**, with a mixture of theater people and eclectic dressers. Although there are a lot of attractive people here, it can be hard to meet new faces since the school is so small."

Q "I've definitely had friends from other schools comment that **Muhlenberg is a hot college**. I guess there are worse things we could be called."

Q "There are a lot of hot people here, but I somehow **always end up hooking up with people at other colleges** because I party there on the weekends a lot. Sometimes, that makes it easier because word can travel fast on campus."

Q "Sometimes it seems like **the people here are either all Abercrombie models** or own the entire line of clothing."

Q "Muhlenberg is definitely a very good-looking campus. It's definitely a prime place to meet your future husband or wife. Plus, **everyone is just so friendly here** and really goes out of their way to get to know you."

Q "Speaking as a girl, I can tell you that **the male population is cute,** friendly, and isn't homogenous at all."

Q "There is a nice selection of guys and girls on campus. There are definitely some really hot girls here. I love the atmosphere at Muhlenberg because **everyone is so nice**. The people are one of the main things I love the most about Muhlenberg."

Q "Sometimes, it seems like it's really hard to find people to date here because **the school is so small**. You start to feel like you know everyone you'd want to date. That's when you need to branch out of your own little group, and then you find out that there really are some hot and nice people that you never thought of before."

The College Prowler Take On...
Guys & Girls

Most people at Muhlenberg will agree that it is an attractive campus. While there are always exceptions, the majority of students seem to be pretty concerned with how they look. Students are either just naturally good looking or take the time to make sure they look presentable before leaving the dorm. Some people have even joked that the college must only let good-looking people attend. Of course, there are those who are not as attractive as others, but your chances of finding hot people are good at the 'Berg. Although there are more girls on campus, the ratio of girls to guys isn't so unbalanced that it creates problems. There is a nice selection of both guys and girls on campus, and the hookup potential is about equal for both sexes.

While you never know what will happen, Muhlenberg can be a good place to look for a random hookup, relationship, or even a future husband or wife. At times, it may seem like all the good ones are taken, but that can happen anywhere. You just need to look in different places. Some people complain about the student population being so small because it can seem limiting, but the small size can also be something positive. Since the school is so small and friendly, it can be easier to get to know people. It's not like at some larger universities where you have a class with someone and start to become interested, but then you never see them again. Chances are, if you want to run into someone at the 'Berg, you will. The size can sometimes become as issue when considering the gossip circle, however. On a small campus, it can become hard to keep your personal life private. It is no secret that random hookups occur on campus with friends or when people cut loose at parties; yet, serious relationships are also quite common.

The College Prowler® Grade on
Guys: A-

A high grade for Guys indicates that the male population on campus is attractive, smart, friendly, and engaging, and that the school has a decent ratio of guys to girls.

The College Prowler® Grade on
Girls: A

A high grade for Girls not only implies that the women on campus are attractive, smart, friendly, and engaging, but also that there is a fair ratio of girls to guys.

Athletics

The Lowdown On...
Athletics

Athletic Division:
NCAA Division III

Conference:
Centennial Conference

School Mascot:
Mule

Fields and Facilities:
Cedarcreek Field
Field House
Memorial Hall
Scotty Wood Stadium/Frank Marino Field
Varsity Field

Men's Varsity Sports:
Baseball
Basketball
Cross-Country
Football
Golf
Lacrosse
Soccer
Tennis
Track (Indoor and Outdoor)
Wrestling

Women's Varsity Sports:
Basketball
Cheerleading
Cross-Country
Field Hockey
Golf
Lacrosse
Soccer
Softball
Tennis
Track (Indoor and Outdoor)
Volleyball

Club Sports:
Cycling
Fencing
Ice Hockey
Rugby
Volleyball

Intramurals:
Air Hockey
Basketball
Billiards
Cross-Country
Floor Hockey
Foosball
Football
Frisbee Golf
Racquetball
Soccer
Softball
Tennis
Volleyball

Best Place to Take a Walk

Cedar Beach Park, Trexler Park, neighborhoods surrounding campus

Getting Tickets

There is no need to buy tickets to sporting events on campus, and they are rarely crowded unless it is a big event like Homecoming.

Most Popular Sports

Football, men's soccer, and women's basketball are among the most popular varsity sports on campus. In actuality, Frisbee golf is definitely one of the top sports on campus, even though it isn't an organized campus sport.

Overlooked Teams

The men's golf team has won four Centennial Conference championships in the past 10 years. This is more than any other sport on campus. Their success, however, is not widely known to most students. There are usually fewer than 10 people on the team, and they only have one home meet during their entire season. Combined with the fact that golf isn't a huge spectator sport, it is easy for this team to go largely unnoticed.

Gyms/Facilities

Life Sports Center

The Life Sports Center is where you can find all of Muhlenberg's sport and fitness facilities. It is the general name given to the building that houses Memorial Hall, the Field House, offices, classrooms, racquetball and squash courts, the pool, and exercise and weight rooms. After being under construction for a year, the new three-story fitness building that is connected to the older sections includes a new weight training area, cardio-fitness area, athletic training facilities, dance and aerobic facilities, and new classrooms. The new Life Sports Center was completed in the fall of 2004.

Memorial Hall

Memorial Hall is where you can find the newly resurfaced and repainted basketball court. This is also where Muhlenberg holds big events like concerts.

Field House

The Field House has an indoor track, basketball and tennis courts, and a 25-meter pool.

Students Speak Out On...
Athletics

> "I wouldn't say that varsity sports are huge here. For the most part, I think people are content playing Frisbee with their friends, or they spend some time at the gym."

Q "**Varsity sports are really not very big** since we are Division III. People come here to be future doctors; they're not usually here to play sports. The biggest varsity sports are probably football, soccer, women's basketball, and rugby. A great deal of the campus participates in IM sports."

Q "I play rugby and tennis for IM. They're not huge on campus, but we have a lot of supporters. The coaches are great, and **it's really nice to feel like part of a team**."

Q "If you know people on the teams, you'll go to a game to cheer them on. If you don't know people playing, **Muhlenberg isn't really a school where you go out to a game** because it's a popular thing to do on the weekends."

Q "I hear that a lot of people participate in IM sports. **Some of our teams are pretty good**, but it's not something we're known for at all."

Q "Varsity sports aren't that big on our campus. I worked at a lot of the games to earn some extra money, and **attendance isn't all that great**."

Q "The school is **pretty supportive of the football team**, and most sports have their own house off campus."

Q "Although sports aren't that big in general, there are some that are more popular. **Some people get into football**."

Q "If you're looking for **somewhere that you can play sports and have fun**, you can do that here. If you're looking for a school that puts a huge emphasis on sports, this probably isn't the right place for you to go."

Q "I don't feel like athletics are all that popular at Muhlenberg, but that may simply be because I don't play. **My dad calls me up to tell me when we win a game**, and always sounds bummed when I have no idea what he's talking about. I feel like a lot of people I know are like that; we're more likely to know the latest show being shown in the Center for the Arts than the score of the big game of the weekend."

Q "**I had hoped to play soccer when I came here**, but I ended up dropping it because I got involved with so many other things. Muhlenberg was appealing to me, though, because I knew I could play competitively, but I wasn't at a school where sports were so important that I wouldn't have fun with it, too. I might try to pick it up again next year."

The College Prowler Take On...
Athletics

In general, people don't come to Muhlenberg for the sports; they are something that you might get involved with because you always played in high school or are looking for something fun to do to stay in shape. The Mules compete in the Centennial Conference with Bryn Mawr, Dickinson, Franklin & Marshall, Gettysburg, Haverford, Johns Hopkins, Swarthmore, Ursinus, Washington, Washington and Lee, and McDaniel. They are members of the National Collegiate Athletic Association Division III and Eastern College Athletic Conference. Muhlenberg's sports are important to the students who play them, but they are largely neglected by the student body unless you have friends on the team. This isn't to say that the teams aren't successful; you just don't typically see them having a huge following on campus. Muhlenberg offers a wide variety of intramurals and club sports, and Frisbee golf is a popular pastime for students.

Sports aren't the main reason you come to Muhlenberg, but that doesn't mean you can't have fun with them. In many cases, the teams probably aren't given the credit that they deserve just because the general student population is unaware of what goes on with them. A lot of times, you are more likely to hear about the latest theatrical production than the game over the weekend. While you probably won't get really into the sports as a spectator, those who play seem to really enjoy it. There are several teams with impressive records, and there is always a lot of fun to be had just by being part of a team.

The College Prowler® Grade on
Athletics: C

A high grade in Athletics indicates that students have school spirit, that sports programs are respected, that games are well-attended, and that intramurals are a prominent part of student life.

Nightlife

The Lowdown On...
Nightlife

Club and Bar Prowler: Popular Nightlife Spots!

Club Crawler:

While Muhlenberg isn't located in the middle of a huge city, there are several clubs that are within a short driving distance. If you head into downtown Allentown, there are a few clubs within minutes of one another. Remember that Philadelphia is just over an hour away, so you can always head into Philly if you find the club scene lacking.

Banana Joe's
318 Hamilton St., Allentown
(610) 776-6476
www.bananajoespa.com

Banana Joe's is one of the most popular places for Muhlenberg students. It's really close and it has a very relaxed atmosphere. It has some great specials including awesome happy hour deals on Friday. The place has two dance floors, pool, food, television, and both indoor and outdoor bars. They feature several bands, DJs who play current radio hits and hip hop, karaoke, and dancers.

The Bar with No Name at the Holiday Inn Bethlehem

Routes 22 & 512, 300 Gateway Dr., Bethlehem
(610) 866-5800

A lot of people don't know about this club because it's located in the Holiday Inn, but it's cool because of its hours and no cover charge. They are open seven days a week and have a happy hour each weeknight, which can be pretty nice if you have random days off during the week. It's more upscale than the other night clubs though, so proper dress is required.

Crocodile Rock Café

520 Hamilton St., Allentown
(610) 434-4600

www.crocodilerockcafe.com

"Croc Rock" offers a variety of types of entertainment because it has several different club floors, an outdoor patio, and a concert hall. The concert hall gets some big bands that you have to buy tickets for, but they also get some really good local bands that are included in the cover charge price. The '80s Retro Room plays your favorites from the '80s, and the Dance Downunder Club has a DJ who plays typical club music.

Main Gate

17th Saint St., Allentown
(610) 776-7711

Main Gate can be a popular spot for Muhlenberg students because it is so close to campus, and they sponsor Muhlenberg nights throughout the year. Some students complain that is has a somewhat sketchy atmosphere, but it can be fun, too.

The Sterling Hotel

341 Hamilton St., Allentown
(610) 433-3480

www.thesterlinghotel.com

The Sterling Hotel is a good place to go if you're looking for food and live music instead of the dance club scene. You can go for dinner, and then stay late to enjoy the bands. Wednesday features an "Open Mic Jam."

Bar Prowler:

Bars are popular places to hang out because there are several that are really close to campus. You don't need to be 21 to get into all of them either, so they can be good for mixed groups of friends. Some people can go to get drinks, and others can go just for the food and atmosphere.

Bethlehem Brew Works

569 Main St., Bethlehem

(610) 882-1300

www.thebrewworks.com

This is a nice place to go for something different because it's located in the Historic District of Bethlehem.

It's open seven days a week and serves both lunch and dinner, in addition to having a bar scene at night. The Steelgaarden is the lounge area and features two pool tables, and really comfortable couches and sofas to kick back and relax. They serve over 100 Belgian bottled beers as well as the beer that is brewed right there on premise.

Chicken Lounge

3245 Hamilton Blvd., Allentown

(610) 439-1707

The Chicken Lounge is a five-minute drive from campus, and it's a popular place to go for snacks and drinks. It may seem sketchy from the outside, but it's really quite cozy and relaxed once you go inside. You can sit at the bar in the center, or chill out at the tables and booths. They have a good variety of food on the menu, but most people will tell you that the nachos are a must for every Chicken Lounge outing!

JP O'Malley's

1528 W Union St.

(610) 821-5556

O'Malley's is very affordable and has over 25 beers on tap. Some find the dark, smokey, wood-paneled interior intimate and inviting, while others find it a little cramped.

Rookie's Restaurant and Sports Pub

1328 W. Tilghman St., Allentown

(610) 821-8484

Rookie's is known as having some of the best wings in the area. They also have three big screen televisions, which makes Rookie's a popular place to watch sporting events.

Other Places to Check Out:
Big Woody's
Buckeye Tavern
Club Liquid
Stooges

What to Do if You're Not 21:

Anylise's Hava Java
526 N 19th St., Allentown
(610) 432-3045

Hava Java's is a cool little café right across the street from the 19th Street Theatre, so it's really convenient if you want to stop in after a show for some dessert. The desserts are really good, and it's a perfect atmosphere for hanging out and chatting. They occasionally have live entertainment, but it tends to feel a little cramped when this is going on.

Borders Books
1937 Whitehall Mall, Whitehall
(610) 432-5520

The café in Borders Books can be a fun place to hang out if you just feel like getting off campus. They have some really good desserts, a variety of hot and cold drinks, and obviously there are plenty of shopping opportunities when you're finished.

Vargtimmen King Koffee
506 Chestnut St., Emmaus
(610) 965-3257

King Koffee is a cute coffeehouse in Emmaus.

Student Favorites:
Banana Joe's
Crocodile Rock

Cheapest Place to Get a Drink:
JP O'Malley's

Favorite Drinking Games:
Beer Pong
Card Games
Quarters
Flip Cup

Useful Resources for Nightlife:
allentown.citysearch.com

Bars Close At:
2 a.m.

Primary Areas with Nightlife:
Downtown Allentown

Organization Parties

Muhlenberg Activities Council (MAC) sponsors parties/dances on campus all the time. They usually have at least one every month in Seegers; sometimes there are even more than this. These parties are whatever you make of them, and it really depends on the crowd that turns out. They can be pretty dead, but you can still have a good time if you go with a group of friends. Most of the people who go are freshmen, since they're on campus and typically don't have access to alcohol. Other groups on campus have their own parties, but these are usually at houses and aren't nearly as publicized. Some campus-sponsored parties are BYOB.

Frats

See the Greek Section.

Students Speak Out On...
Nightlife

> "Muhlenberg is not a school for big parties, but small gatherings of friends are common. This can actually be more fun, depending on the type of atmosphere you typically like."

Q "The parties are pretty good, especially once you're a sophomore. I personally like house parties the best, which I attended more this year than last because I knew more people. I think it's important to make it clear that **if you're looking for a party school**, Muhlenberg is not the right place for you. If you want to have a good time and like chilling with friends, then it's great."

Q "At Muhlenberg, **you usually make your own party**, but fraternities do hit it big with Halloween, Mardi Gras, and Beach Bash. The clubs are pretty good; Main Gate occasionally sponsors nights that are just for Muhlenberg [students]."

Q "The parties on campus are **pretty good**. I especially like the theme parties."

Q "Muhlenberg is not a party school, but there is always something to do if you look for it. **The athletic houses have parties a lot**, and there are parties in the MILE houses. Also, Sigma Phi Epsilon has dance parties, as well as regular Thursday and Saturday night parties. Benfer, South, and Robertson are all considered pretty social dorms as well. The nearest club is Maingate, which is good for dancing and drinks."

Q "I hear **Banana Joe's is good**. I'm excited to go there for the drinks, appetizers, live music, and dancing."

Q "The parties are available on the weekends if that's what you want, but there is **always something to do** if that's not your style. I enjoy spending my weekends between a mix of going to parties and just hanging out with friends."

Q **"There really aren't that many clubs in Allentown.** I heard they just opened a club downtown, and there's always Main Gate, which I'm not really a big fan of. I don't really frequent the Greek parties, but Phi Kappa Tau's are always fun because the brothers are all really cool. I usually end up just hanging out with friends because parties aren't really my scene."

Q "Some people complain that Muhlenberg isn't a big party school, but I definitely feel like you can make it what you want it to be. If you're looking for a party, you'll be able to find one. You can also have a great time just hanging out in the dorms. **There are some bars and clubs in the area**. A lot of people go to Big Woody's because it's really close, or the Chicken Lounge is good for drinks and nachos."

Q "If I really want to go to a good club, I'll **go into Philly**. If I'm just looking for something fun to do that will get us off campus, though, there are several clubs in Allentown that are fun and close."

Q "Muhlenberg Activities Committee (MAC) really tries to offer students alternatives to frat parties and just hanging in the dorm. They sponsor parties at least once a month, but whether you have fun at them really depends on what you're looking for and if your friends go to them. **Sometimes they can be pretty dead**; if you bring a group of friends with you, they can be a lot of fun."

Q "I love going to Croc Rock with my friends because it offers a good variety. **I go for the bands**, and they go for the dancing."

The College Prowler Take On...
Nightlife

Muhlenberg is not particularly known for being a big party school, but that doesn't mean that it's all work and no play on campus either! It seems like a lot of students at Muhlenberg are perfectly content making their own fun with small groups of friends around campus or just hanging out in the dorms. For those who are looking for alternatives to this type of low-key entertainment, campus parties and clubs do offer a variety of other options. As students get older, these options become greater. At first, freshmen stick to the organized MAC events on the weekends. After the first couple of weeks, frats open their doors to freshmen, though it isn't always easy for guys to gain access without knowing someone who lives in the house. After freshman year, the frats seem to lose their novelty for many (unless you are friends with the guys in the frat or have gone Greek yourself). House parties become more popular as you get to know more people who live in MILE houses, the new dorms, or off campus.

Once students turn 21, clubs and bars in the area become the choice destinations. While Allentown doesn't have as many clubs as Philadelphia or New York, there are several places in the area that offer good drinks and entertainment. Crocodile Rock and Banana Joe's are two of the most popular places for Muhlenberg students, and the Chicken Lounge offers great snacks. You don't always need to be 21, and there are also quite a few coffee shops in the area.

The College Prowler® Grade on
Nightlife: C+

A high grade in Nightlife indicates that there are many bars and clubs in the area that are easily accessible and affordable. Other determining factors include the number of options for the under-21 crowd and the prevalence of house parties.

Greek Life

The Lowdown On...
Greek Life

Number of Fraternities:
4

Number of Sororities:
4

Undergrad Men in Fraternities:
19%

Undergrad Women in Sororities:
20%

Fraternities on Campus:
Alpha Epsilon Pi
Delta Tau Delta
Phi Kappa Tau
Sigma Phi Epsilon

Sororities on Campus:
Alpha Chi Omega
Delta Zeta
Phi Mu
Phi Sigma Sigma

Other Greek Organizations:
Panhellenic Council
Interfraternity Council

Did You Know?

Muhlenberg does not allow its students to "go Greek" **until their sophomore year**.

Each spring semester, the fraternities and sororities compete in a number of events during Greek Week.

Students Speak Out On...
Greek Life

> "I have friends who are Greek and friends who are independent; it doesn't really seem to make a difference."

Q "I'm not Greek, and I have a great social life. **The only time that it really bothered me was during pledging** because a lot of my friends weren't around. It's a great scene for some people, and it just doesn't work for others."

Q "I decided not to become a part of the Greek life and still have friends who are **very involved with their frats and sororities**. If anything, it has expanded my circle of friends, and I don't feel like I am missing out on anything."

Q "Greek life can definitely dominate the social scene at times. The cliques made through Greek life are **actually pretty nauseating**."

Q "The Greeks bring an aspect to student life that is quite different from the other organizations. This is neither good nor bad. Although they provide social scenes, **there are many other things to do on campus** than go to a frat on a Saturday night."

Q "Greek life can be big, but it doesn't totally dominate the social scene on campus. If you want to party frequently, don't mind the prospect of paying for friends or spending **a semester of your life doing the bidding of other people**, then Greek life is for you. Some Greek organizations perform worthwhile community service, which is a plus, and it will hopefully become more frequent."

Q "There seems to be a big group of **people who revolve their lives around Greek life**, another group who is not involved but frequent the parties, and then everyone else just seems to float around."

Q "Greek life definitely doesn't dominate the social scene. This is partly due to the fact that **students aren't allowed to pledge until their sophomore year**, which I think is a great idea. This allows potential pledges to really settle themselves into college life, both academically and socially."

Q "Greek life is what you want it to be. If you plan on pledging and becoming involved in it, it can easily become the main thing in your life on campus. If you want to join and still do other things, you can do that. Lastly, there are plenty of people on campus who have **nothing to do with Greek life** and still have a great time."

Q "To people who are Greek, **it dominates the social scene**. If you're not part of that, you can go through college without ever feeling like you missed out on anything. It's all up to the individual person."

Q "**Greek life can be big**, but it's not like at some schools where you don't even talk to people who are in other sororities. It is quite possible for girls in different sororities to live together and get along just fine."

Q "It can be **great for people who like to party a lot** because you have a set group of friends that pretty much are forced to hang out with you. You won't feel like you are lacking a social life if you don't join though."

The College Prowler Take On...
Greek Life

Those who have decided to go Greek at Muhlenberg feel that it has been great for their social life, and it has made a big difference in their college experience. They have made great friends and have opportunities to participate in a variety of activities on campus. Those who don't belong to a fraternity or sorority are usually pretty indifferent to Greek life. Since Muhlenberg does not allow freshmen to pledge, exposure to Greek life as a freshman mainly consists of parties. A lot of freshmen, especially girls, like to make their way over to the frat houses for the dance parties. After freshman year, the Greek impact on students' social scene seems to die down, unless you or your friends decide to become a part of it by pledging. A fair percentage of the campus belongs to a fraternity or a sorority, but it's not very exclusive. Students don't feel pressured to join in order to make friends, and most Greek events are open to the entire campus. Most students will agree that their social lives have not been greatly impacted by their decision not to join.

If you've always been interested in joining a Greek organization, Muhlenberg's Greek life has a lot to offer. Fraternities and sororities perform community service in various ways on campus, but they are typically known for Greek Week and the parties. The frats hit it big with events such as Mardi Gras and Beach Bash. The outcome of Greek Week events doesn't really matter to most on campus, but everyone knows it's going on because of all of the people in matching shirts for an entire week.

The College Prowler® Grade on
Greek Life: B+

A good grade means that Greek life has a highly-visible role on campus. The poorer the grade, the less prominent the Greek scene.

Drug Scene

The Lowdown On...
Drug Scene

Most Prevalent Drugs on Campus:
Alcohol
Marijuana

Liquor-Related Referrals:
304

Liquor-Related Arrests:
22

Drug-Related Referrals:
21

Drug-Related Arrests:
0

Students Speak Out On...
Drug Scene

> "There really isn't a huge drug scene at Muhlenberg. I mean, we do have our 'pot heads,' but I wouldn't say that it is very prevalent on the campus."

Q "The drug scene is pretty big; **a lot of people smoke marijuana**. People do other drugs, but that isn't too big."

Q "I don't do drugs, and I have never felt the pressure to do them here. I do know of students who are involved in that 'scene,' but **it is done quietly**. I do not believe that it affects the overall college atmosphere at all."

Q "Drugs are available if you're interested, but if you're not, **you wouldn't even know they were here**."

Q "Lot's of people smoke weed, but it's not a constant presence on campus at all. **Most of it goes on off campus**, as far as I know. I've never been exposed to heavier drugs here, so if it goes on, it is pretty well hidden."

Q "I see very little drug use on campus, much less than my high school. **There is no peer pressure**."

Q "**People smoke weed**. That's all I've ever heard. I don't think people use hard drugs here."

Q "**We all know drugs are on our campus,** but it really doesn't seem to be a huge problem. It's very hush-hush."

Q "I'd say **you could get pot if you wanted it**, but I don't see it as a big issue."

Q "There really is **no presence of hard drugs**. Marijuana is present just like at any other college, but no more than any of the other schools I've visited."

Q "I hear about and have seen people smoking marijuana, but I've never been pressured to do it. I think it's one of those things that if you want drugs, you definitely can get them, but if you don't, it's no big deal. **They're not shoved in your face everywhere you go**. No one will try to push it on you."

Q "**In three years, I've never once been offered drugs** or felt like it was a pressure. Like most schools, I'm sure it's available if you're into that. It's just not something that you need to deal with if it's not for you."

The College Prowler Take On...
Drug Scene

If you're not into drugs, it's possible to go through your four years at Muhlenberg without ever even encountering them. Sure, there are drugs on campus; it's just not something that is very prevalent within everyday activities on campus. It seems like people who smoke pot tend to find one another, but it's not like they come and recruit users. The only people who are very aware of the existence of a drug scene are those who are a part of it; for other people, you can go about your life without having it really impact your college experience.

In many respects, Muhlenberg probably has fewer students using drugs than a typical high school. The only drug that you see on a somewhat regular basis is alcohol, but that is to be expected at most colleges. The faculty has started to get worried about the rise in alcohol on campus in the past couple of years, but the majority of students don't seem to think that it's that out of hand. One thing that most students tend to agree on when it comes to drugs on campus is that there really isn't a pressure to try them. If you decide that you want to use them, they're available. If you don't, people leave you alone.

The College Prowler® Grade on Drug Scene: B

A good grade means that drugs are not a highly-visible threat on campus. The poorer the grade, the more prominent the drug scene.

Campus Strictness

The Lowdown On...
Campus Strictness

What Are You Most Likely to Get Caught Doing on Campus?

- Parking illegally
- Too much noise in the dorms
- Candles or incense in the dorms
- Drinking underage
- Displaying bottles or drinking trophies in the dorm

Students Speak Out On...
Campus Strictness

> "Campus police seem reasonable. People caught breaking the rules suffer consequences like classes concerning substance abuse, but nothing seems too severe."

Q "They say they're really strict, but they are actually very lax. You can get tons of warnings. I know people who have been busted, but they seem to take it as a joke because **the campus police aren't amazingly strict.**"

Q "Campus police can be strict if they catch you being totally stupid. **You won't have any problems** if you're responsible."

Q "Campus police are pretty strict about freshmen drinking; they've been known to bust up quite a few parties. At the same time, no one pretends that Muhlenberg is a dry campus. Students who are over 21 are allowed to have alcohol in their rooms. **The school seems to recognize that college is college**, and that students are going to drink. They try to promote responsibility."

Q "If you are smart about where and when you drink and **don't create a scene**, the campus police don't greatly interfere with our lives."

Q "A lot of people get away with things, but campus police are pretty strict about drugs and drinking if they actually catch you. You will probably get a fine and have to go to **seminars about drinking and drugs** the first time. Then, after that, you might get suspended for a semester."

Q "Just be smart, and **you won't get in trouble**."

Q "I find that **our school can be really inconsistent**. I know some people do things all the time and never get caught; there are other people who get in trouble for really dumb things."

Q "There was **a lot of complaining last year** about police being too strict, but people seem to be less upset about that this year. I'm not really into drinking, so I've never had to deal with it."

Q "I've never had any problems with campus police. Some people complain, but **if you get busted, it's probably your own fault**. I feel like you have to be pretty dumb for them to really give you a hard time."

Q "Every once in a while, the school will really crack down. Like **this past year, there were some problems** with a lot of freshmen going overboard with drinking. When it comes to that though, wouldn't we rather them be strict than see a bunch of freshmen killing themselves?"

Q "It's a college. Campus police know that students are going to be exposed to alcohol. They know we are going to have nights where we get really loud even though it's late at night. You just have to be smart about it. **If they tell you to stop, listen to them**. If you're a jerk, they'll bust you whenever they can."

The College Prowler Take On...
Campus Strictness

While some students complain that campus police are out to catch students, most feel that their punishments are fair. There are stories about people being angry because they got fined for having empty bottles or shot glasses in their room, but this typically only happens to people who are also getting busted for other things. Students need to be smart about what they do; if you're going to be involved in things that you know you could get in trouble for, don't advertise it. If you keep your door shut and keep the noise to a minimum, it's rare that campus police will give you a hard time. Also, remember to remove anything from your dorms that could give campus police a reason to fine you before going home on breaks. While it's not very likely that it will be spotted, there is always a chance that the wrong person might see it.

Students should remember that campus police are there to protect them, not to look for ways to bust them. Recently, there has been some concern on campus about the rise in alcohol use among freshmen. For this reason, campus police seem to have been increasing their surveillance of the freshman dorms. Overall, the college seems to recognize that college is a place where students are going to test their freedom. They are there to step in when it's needed, but they also give students some leeway.

The College Prowler® Grade on

Campus Strictness: B

A high Campus Strictness grade implies an overall lenient atmosphere; police and RAs are fairly tolerant, and the administration's rules are flexible.

Parking

The Lowdown On...
Parking

MC Parking Services:
Campus Safety
(484) 664-3112
www.muhlenberg.edu/mgt/police

Student Parking Lot?
Yes

Freshmen Allowed to Park?
No

Approximate Parking Permit Cost:
$25

Common Parking Tickets:
No Parking Zone: $20
Handicapped Zone: $50
Fire Lane: $50

Parking Permits

It's relatively easy to get a parking permit. During the first few days of the year, you will see signs listing the dates and times to register and buy a permit. There is no need to apply; everyone who is an upperclassman can get a permit if they fill out the form and pay the $25. Just take your student ID and car registration and insurance information to campus safety in the basement of Prosser. They will give you a colored sticker to put on your car; you are allowed to park in specific lots depending on the color of your sticker.

Did You Know?

Best Places to Find a Parking Spot
- East lot
- Liberty Street

Good Luck Getting a Parking Spot Here!
- Chew Street
- South and Robertson lots

Students Speak Out On...
Parking

> "Parking totally depends on luck. Sometimes it's no problem; other times, I can drive around for 15 minutes before I find a spot that I can park in legally."

Q "Parking stinks, but show me a campus where it doesn't! **Freshmen can't have cars**, and upperclassmen have to hope to find a spot in a parking lot so they don't have to parallel park on the street somewhere. Parking permits are pretty cheap, though, which is a bonus."

Q "Parking isn't great. Freshmen aren't allowed to have cars, mostly because of the lack of space. In addition, while you pay money for a parking sticker, it doesn't mean that you're guaranteed a spot in a lot. All in all, **it can be one heck of a headache**."

Q "Parking is very cheap at Muhlenberg. It only costs about $25 for a full year of parking, and I have friends at other schools who pay $100 per semester to park! The problem at Muhlenberg is that campus safety gives everyone a parking sticker without counting how many spots are available. This can cause some problems (especially by the dorms that are mostly for seniors), but **I've never had a big problem finding a spot**. There's always street parking. Muhlenberg has also been working on expanding parking to meet the greater demand."

Q "It can be **pretty easy to park** if you're aware of your options."

Q "Parking is actually pretty difficult. There are **too many students with cars** and not enough parking spots."

Q "**Parking is horrible**. Don't even get me started."

Q "Parking has been fine overall for me. There have only been a few times that I haven't been able to find a spot in a lot, and then I just go to the street. **Learn to parallel park**—it will help you immensely!"

Q "It is definitely not easy to park here! Parking spaces are not easy to come by, so when you find one, you do not want to move! The good thing, though, is that **the parking pass is so inexpensive** compared to other schools."

Q "Because it is such a small school, there is **not a lot of parking**. Freshmen aren't supposed to bring cars, but a lot of them bring them anyway. Parking is limited, but there are so many residential streets surrounding the campus that you can always park on the street and be fairly safe."

Q "**We definitely need more parking** on campus, but I hear that we're working on it."

The College Prowler Take On...
Parking

Parking is probably among the biggest complaints about the Muhlenberg campus. As a freshman, you are not technically allowed to bring cars onto campus without getting special permission from the director of campus safety. Some people are able to get this by claiming that they need a car for health reasons or in order to get to a job they already have. To legally have a car on campus, you need to register your car and pay a registration fee. The fee is $25 for the year, so at least it is not too expensive. At registration, you are given a parking permit which is a specifically colored sticker which corresponds with specific lots on campus that you are allowed to park in.

Unfortunately, not all of the dorms have lots near them. However, the campus is small, so it is rare that the lot would be more than a few minutes' walk. Just because you have a sticker does not mean you are guaranteed a spot in one of the lots. After your first year, the school doesn't do anything to limit the number of cars on campus, resulting in far more cars than spaces. Depending on the time of day, it is quite possible that you will find yourself circling the lots, looking for spots for up to 15 minutes before you either get lucky or make the decision to chance a ticket by parking somewhere else, like the street. The worst time of the year for parking is during the winter because there are certain streets that you cannot park on with snow, and the snow always ends up taking up spots in the lots.

The College Prowler® Grade on
Parking: C

A high grade in this section indicates that parking is both available and affordable, and that parking enforcement isn't overly severe.

Transportation

The Lowdown On...
Transportation

Ways to Get Around Town:

On Campus

The Muhlenberg Shuttle

Hours: Wednesday 6 p.m.–10 p.m., Friday 6 p.m.–1 a.m., Saturday 1 p.m.–1 a.m., Sunday 1 p.m.–8 p.m.

Steve Goosley, Shuttle Coordinator

shuttlesteve51@msn.com

(610) 417-1057

The shuttle takes students to many of the popular areas in Allentown including the Lehigh Valley Mall, the Rose Bowl Bowling Alley, and several shopping centers and restaurants. The shuttle departs from the circle outside Seegers Union 10 minutes after the hour. If you don't see the shuttle there, look in front of the Center for the Arts.

Public Transportation
Trans Bridge Lines Inc.
(610) 435-8437

Taxi Cabs
Quick Service Taxi
(610) 434-8132

Lehigh Valley Taxi
(610) 867-5855

Car Rentals
Alamo, local: (610) 264-5535
national: (800) 327-9633
www.alamo.com

Avis
local: (610) 264-4450
national: (800) 831-2847
www.avis.com

Budget
local: (610) 266-0667
national: (800) 527-0700
www.budget.com

Dollar
local: (610) 231-8785
national: (800) 800-4000
www.dollar.com

Enterprise
local: (610) 266-4081
national: (800) 736-8222
www.enterprise.com

Hertz
local: (610) 264-4571
national: (800) 654-3131
www.hertz.com

National
local: (610) 264-5535
national: (800) 227-7368
www.nationalcar.com

Best Ways to Get Around Town
Take the Muhlenberg Shuttle

Make friends with people who have cars

Bring a bike

Wear comfortable sneakers

Ways to Get Out of Town:

Airlines Serving Allentown
American Airlines
(800) 433-7300
www.americanairlines.com

Continental
(800) 523-3273
www.continental.com

Delta
(800) 221-1212
www.delta.com

Northwest
(800) 225-2525
www.nwa.com

United
(800) 241-6522
www.united.com

US Airways
(800) 428-4322
www.usairways.com

Airport
Lehigh Valley International Airport, (800) FLY-LVIA

The Lehigh Valley Airport is 9.25 miles and approximately a 15-minute drive from Muhlenberg College.

How to get to the Airport

The best way to get to the airport from campus is to contact "Shuttle" Steve Goosely and set up details with him.

Shuttlesteve51@msn.com
(610) 417-1057

A cab ride to the airport costs $25, but you can call Shuttle Steve and he'll cut you a deal.

If you can't use Steve, then you can call any of the taxi companies in the area.

Greyhound

The Greyhound Bus Terminal is in Bethlehem, approximately 13 miles from campus. For information, call
(610) 867-3988.

Travel Agents

AAA East Penn
1020 Hamilton St.
Allentown
(610) 434-5141

Students Speak Out On...
Transportation

> "I've never used Allentown public transportation. I find that it's pretty easy to find someone with a car who is willing to take you somewhere."

Q "I used to use the campus shuttle a lot; **it can be really convenient** when you don't have a car available."

Q "There's **a bus station nearby and an airport**, but there's no convenient train station. This stinks if you want an easy way into Philly. The campus shuttle is probably the best way around without a car."

Q "If you don't have a car, **make friends with people who have cars**. It makes things so much easier."

Q "A lot of people complain that **public transportation can be a pain** from here. I have my own car, and I love not having to rely on anyone else for rides."

Q "Freshman year, most people are in the same boat you are. **You can bond over taking the shuttle together**. After that, it's nice to have a car or know someone who has a car on campus. Keep in mind that there are a lot of places near enough that you can always walk, too. Sometimes, it's fun to walk even if you have a car."

Q "The college **offers a shuttle to take kids around town**. It will take you pretty much anywhere you'd want to go in the Lehigh Valley, and it's much cheaper than calling a cab."

Q "There is a Muhlenberg Shuttle, which is very convenient. It operates until pretty late on the weekends, and it will take you to **all of the popular attractions**."

Q **"Shuttle Steve is willing to take you around** pretty much wherever you please. The Lehigh Valley International Airport is nearby. Also, asking upperclassmen for rides is fairly reliable."

Q "I really don't know much about public transportation in Allentown. I felt like I was really pushed to either stay on campus or take the Muhlenberg Shuttle my freshman year. This isn't bad because there's **a lot of free stuff to do on campus**, and a lot of freshmen stay around on the weekends. After I had my car on campus, I started to go out a lot more."

The College Prowler Take On...
Transportation

The most common mode of mass transportation used at Muhlenberg is the Muhlenberg Shuttle. A lot of people resort to taking the shuttle as freshmen because it's cheap, convenient, and will take you to the well-known areas of Allentown. Although, it can be a little embarrassing to arrive in the shuttle, you do what you have to do. It's also more fun if you go with a group of people; then you're not the only one getting out of the vehicle. After being on campus for a while, you'll meet people who have cars. This is obviously preferred over taking the red van or yellow school bus. As far as public transportation goes, most students stay away from it, with the exception of the airport. The Lehigh Valley International Airport is very convenient as it only takes about 15 minutes by car to reach it.

Public transportation is not widely used at Muhlenberg because it isn't very convenient for most students. The bus and train stations are not within a close distance, so you would usually need to find some type of transportation just to get to them. Because of this, most people only use buses and trains when they need to get out of Allentown and don't want to fly. Most people either have cars or know people who have cars. If you don't have access to a car, plan on walking or hanging out with Shuttle Steve.

The College Prowler® Grade on
Transportation: C+

A high grade for Transportation indicates that campus buses, public buses, cabs, and rental cars are readily-available and affordable. Other determining factors include proximity to an airport and the necessity of transportation.

Weather

The Lowdown On...
Weather

Average Temperature:
Fall: 52°F
Winter: 30°F
Spring: 49°F
Summer: 72°F

Average Precipitation:
Fall: 3.8 in.
Winter: 3.2 in.
Spring: 3.8 in.
Summer: 4.1 in.

Students Speak Out On...
Weather

> "I always joke that Muhlenberg in the spring is how I always envisioned college. Looking out on the lawn and seeing so many people out there studying or playing Frisbee—it's just like a brochure."

Q "The weather is moderate. **Bring a variety of clothes** like pants and sweaters for the winter and shorts and T-shirts for the spring and fall."

Q "It's hot in the summer, and it's cold in the winter. It's perfect, if you ask me! There is **nothing like watching the seasons change at Muhlenberg**! In the fall, leaves cover Academic Row; during the first days of spring, everyone is outside doing work or just enjoying the sun. Bring clothes you can have fun in after you get back from class."

Q "The winters are snowy, and the springs are beautiful. **We cover all the seasons** to their stereotypical descriptions."

Q "The **winter is always a bit chilly**, and it may snow, but not so much that you're going to need a plow to get out of the dorm."

Q "**Snow in April**! Yeah, we've had that here. That's crazy if you ask me, but it's not just here. They got snow really late at my house, too. Other than that, the weather's fine. We have a nice balance of having all of the seasons."

Q "I'd recommend snow boots in the winter, and a blanket to sit on outside in the sun. **Expect snow in the winter and to sweat in the summer**, and bring a fan."

Q "The weather changes drastically with the seasons. I would bring clothes for every type of weather. In August and September, it can be pretty hot. In the winter, **it gets pretty cold and sometimes snows**. The past few years, we've had some major snow as late as April. I would be prepared for anything. It's also good to know that Muhlenberg's located in a valley, so it's windy almost all of the time."

Q "The beginning and end of the school year are hot, especially if you don't have air-conditioning in your dorm. **Winters aren't exactly sub-zero**, but they're not warm, either. It usually snows, which makes for some great sledding and some hilarious anatomically correct snowmen."

Q "We don't go to school in sunny Florida, and we don't have amazing snow for skiing. Allentown does have a good balance of everything in between, though. You'll have some hot days and some cold. It will rain, and it'll be sunny. **You should come prepared for it all**."

Q "The weather here is the same as it was at my home. Sometimes, we're a few degrees cooler because we're in a valley, but **overall, it's nothing special**. The weather here is typical Pennsylvania weather, I guess."

The College Prowler Take On...
Weather

The weather in Allentown fits the stereotypical descriptions of the four seasons. It's nice to see how the campus looks different as the seasons change. Walking down Academic Row, you can see how the trees lining the walkway change color throughout the year. You'll need to bundle up in the winter, and you'll sweat in the summer. Fall and spring are really nice because they fall pleasantly in between the two extremes. It's nice that campus is so small when bad weather hits because you really don't need to walk very far to get to anything you need. When it's nice out, the whole campus just seems busier and more alive. You'll see crowds of people hanging out, or eating at the tables in Parents Plaza, and a lot of people go out on the lawn to do work, play games, or just relax on blankets.

When packing for the climate, you should bring a range of clothing. You will want everything from shorts and tank tops, to heavy coats and gloves. If you aren't lucky enough to be in a dorm with air-conditioning, you will definitely want to bring a fan for the beginning and end of the year. While some places can claim that they have a dry heat, Allentown's summers are hot and humid. This can make the dorms quite sticky. With the exception of some fluke snowstorms that came really late these past couple of years, the snow isn't usually too bad. You'll be cold walking to class, but you don't usually need to worry about being snowed in.

The College Prowler® Grade on
Weather: C+

A high Weather grade designates that temperatures are mild and rarely reach extremes, that the campus tends to be sunny rather than rainy, and that weather is fairly consistent rather than unpredictable.

MUHLENBERG COLLEGE
Report Card Summary

B+ ACADEMICS

C+ LOCAL ATMOSPHERE

A SAFETY & SECURITY

B- COMPUTERS

A- FACILITIES

B+ CAMPUS DINING

C+ OFF-CAMPUS DINING

B+ CAMPUS HOUSING

C+ OFF-CAMPUS HOUSING

D- DIVERSITY

A- GUYS

A GIRLS

C ATHLETICS

C+ NIGHTLIFE

B+ GREEK LIFE

B DRUG SCENE

B CAMPUS STRICTNESS

C PARKING

C+ TRANSPORTATION

C+ WEATHER

Overall Experience

Students Speak Out On...
Overall Experience

> "The people are great, the professors are amazing, and the campus is so beautiful. I'm definitely very happy to be here, and I can't imagine being anywhere else."

Q "Muhlenberg is **a great choice if you're looking for a small school**. If not, you may not be happy with your choice."

Q "Overall, **my years at Muhlenberg have been an incredible experience**. The friendly atmosphere is apparent from the moment you step on campus."

Q "I can't picture myself going to any other school. Sometimes **I wish Muhlenberg was a little bigger**, but that would be my only real complaint."

Q "Overall, I really like it here. The people I've met have been amazing, and I was able to make friends really fast. The campus is so small that **you never feel like just one of the crowd**. I really believe that everyone has a chance to shine here. Even though Muhlenberg may not be the biggest party school, I have had some of the most fun in my life just doing random things with friends. The college experience here is what you make of it. So far, it has been something I will always remember as being one of the best experiences of my life."

Q "I love Muhlenberg and feel that it has so much to offer, especially if students take advantage of all of the opportunities here. **The environment is warm and comfortable**, and I have great friends who are so supportive. I truly believe that there is something for everyone here, and there is no place that I would rather be."

Q "I think I made a great choice coming to Muhlenberg. There is **a great balance between education and fun**; you just have to find your niche. Muhlenberg is very fun, and the education is excellent."

Q "The fact that we are so small can be annoying at times. Sometimes, I wish I had chosen a larger university; yet, I know that **I'd miss the personal attention I get here**. So overall, I'm happy. You just need to decide what matters to you the most and then weigh your options."

Q "Some people count down the days until they graduate with excitement because they cannot wait to be finished with school; I tend to avoid thinking about how many days are left because **I dread leaving Muhlenberg**!"

Q "**I only applied to one school, Muhlenberg**, and I do not regret my decision at all! I am going into my senior year, and I could not imagine being anywhere else. I am going to come out with friendships with friends and also professors. My time at Muhlenberg will not only be the best four years of my life, it will also be the most valuable and missed."

Q "I applied to Muhlenberg early decision, and I have never regretted it. I can't imagine enjoying college anywhere else as much as I have enjoyed my time here. As corny as it may sound, the 'Berg truly is a 'Caring College.' My years here have **allowed me to grow intellectually and professionally** in a supportive and friendly environment."

Q "I love Muhlenberg! I have never regretted coming here, and I would never turn back. The learning is fun, and the experience and memories are unforgettable. Walking down Academic Row, people shout out your name as you look around and see a beautiful campus with students studying on the grass, playing games, or eating. **It feels like something from a movie**, but then you realize that you picked an awesome college because Muhlenberg is real!"

Q "I love Muhlenberg; they don't call it the 'Caring College' for nothing. Students are given plenty of independence and opportunities, yet they know that there are people surrounding them who will support them and care about them. If you want to feel like you're in a place 'where everybody knows your name,' then come to Muhlenberg. **There's no where else I'd want to be**. Muhlenberg has nurtured my development as an intellectual, activist, and adult. It has helped me to become the person I want to be."

Q "My experience at Muhlenberg has been a combination of academic enrichment, genuine delight, cherished moments, **totally unforeseen opportunities**, endless possibilities, and deliciously pleasurable and beautiful experiences."

Q "Muhlenberg was my first choice, and **I've never once looked back**. I love the campus, the size, the students, and the faculty. In fact, leaving Muhlenberg will be a very difficult ordeal for me."

The College Prowler Take On...
Overall Experience

Although you may hear some grumbling around campus during registration, or the housing lottery, the overwhelming majority of students are eager to praise their experience at Muhlenberg. The academics at Muhlenberg are top notch, but it is the combination of these academic opportunities with the inviting and supportive atmosphere that really makes students feel that they made the right choice in coming to the 'Berg. While some students complain about the small size, other students attribute a lot of Muhlenberg's appeal to its feeling of a close community. Although the party scene may not be as wild as it is at some colleges, most students will tell you that there is always something to do on the weekends.

While no college experience can be completely flawless, most students claim that they can't see themselves being happier anywhere else. The work can be challenging at times, but you know that you will step into your future feeling as prepared as possible. You will be encouraged to think independently and become actively engaged in whatever you are studying. This isn't a place where you can sit back and coast through the next four years, but it's difficult to even be tempted to do that when you are surrounded by so many people who are passionate about what they are doing. It's also a huge source of comfort to know that there are always people behind you every step of the way.

The Inside Scoop

The Lowdown On...
The Inside Scoop

Muhlenberg Slang:

Know the slang, know the school. The following is a list of things you really need to know before coming to Muhlenberg. The more of these words you know, the better off you'll be.

Academic Row – The main walkway where the majority of the academic buildings are located.

Action Station – Area in GQ where something different is offered depending on the day of the week.

Bagel bombs – Bagels with fried egg and cheese from GQ.

The 'Berg – Nickname for Muhlenberg.

The Bubble – Trexler Pavilion or Muhlenberg campus in general.

CA – Baker Center for the Arts.

The Caring College – Nickname for Muhlenberg.

Eastie Beasties – Big bugs that are commonly spotted in East Hall.

The Fish Bowl – Trexler Pavilion.

Fro yo – Frozen yogurt from Garden Room.

General Pete – Statue across from Haas of John Peter Gabriel Muhlenberg who was with George Washington through the famous winter of Valley Forge.

GQ – General's Quarters.

GR – Garden Room.

ML – Martin Luther Hall.

Muhley World – Nickname for Muhlenberg because of its tendency to seem almost too ideal at times.

Napkin Board – Bulletin board in Garden Room where people post napkins with comments.

The New Dorms – South and Robertson Halls.

OCDP – Office of Career Development and Placement, where you go for help with writing resumes or getting internships and jobs.

OIT – Office of Information Technology. They will help you with your computer problems.

Parents Plaza – The area outside of Seegers Union with benches and tables.

Shuttle Steve – Steve Goosley, the man in charge of the campus shuttle.

Swipe – A unit on your meal plan equivalent to one entry into Garden Room or $4.10 in GQ.

The Turtle – Statue in Parents Plaza of a species of bog turtle named after naturalist Gotthilf Henry Ernest Muhlenberg.

Victor's Lament – Big red sculpture on the front lawn.

Things I Wish I Knew Before Coming to MC

- Bring a fan.
- For extra long beds, you only need an extra long fitted sheet.
- Bring shower shoes.
- Time management.
- College classes are a lot more work than in high school.
- How much I'd rely on phone cards and the Internet.

Tips to Succeed at MC

- Make an effort to get to know your professors.
- Get involved with activities.
- Learn how to manage your time.
- Actually go to class because professors will notice.
- Take classes that are taught by professors you like.
- Don't be afraid to ask questions.
- Check your e-mail multiple times each day.

Muhlenberg Urban Legends

- Robertson is haunted by the ghost of a former member of the Muhlenberg faculty whose house was torn down to build the new dorms.
- The Gabriel House, the building that is now used for Muhlenberg's night school, is haunted by the ghost of an African American man who is believed to have once been a Muhlenberg maintenance man.
- A bat affectionately named Bernard lives in the chapel and frequently makes appearances during the Candlelight Carols each December.
- There are many stories about what Victor's Lament actually is supposed to be. Some say that it's a war veteran rising from a wheelchair, and others say that it looks like a large letter M when seen from an airplane.
- The Muhlenberg mascot was almost a turtle because of the species of bog turtle named after naturalist Gotthilf Henry Ernest Muhlenberg.

School Spirit

The overwhelming majority of students at Muhlenberg have a strong sense of school pride and are usually eager to tell others about how much they like it at Muhlenberg. The tour guides do not get paid, yet a number of students are turned down for this position each year because so many students want to be tour guides. Since sports aren't huge here, Homecoming is probably the biggest sporting event that students get into supporting. A lot of people come out to support the school and their peers for other events on campus, though. The bookstore sells just about anything you could want in terms of Muhlenberg gear, and just about everyone owns Muhlenberg clothing.

Traditions

Candlelight Carols

Candlelight Carols services have been a Muhlenberg tradition since 1958. Held in Egner Memorial Chapel the weekend before finals during the fall semester, this beautiful service features performances from the Muhlenberg College Choir, along with student and faculty readings. Tickets are free, but seating is limited so you need to turn in a lottery form.

Geek Week

The fraternities and sororities have Greek Week, and the academic clubs have Geek Week! Different academic clubs on campus have the option of entering their club in this week of different competitions between the clubs on campus.

Jefferson Field Day

Each year, the Friday after the last day of classes is Jefferson Field Day. Students from Jefferson Elementary School in Allentown join students on campus for a day of track and field events. A huge number of Muhlenberg students and faculty spend the day running and helping out with the event. It's a great way to have some fun with kids before starting to study for finals.

Marathon Theatre

During a weekend in the fall semester, members of the Muhlenberg Theatre Association participate in Marathon Theatre. For 24 hours, they put on short dance numbers and skits in order to raise money for different charities. The event takes place in Parents Plaza, so it's fun to stop by and watch on your way in and out of Seegers.

Midnight Breakfast

Muhlenberg has recently started a new tradition during finals week at the end of the year. On the Friday night that begins the weekend before finals, Garden Room hosts a free breakfast at midnight for students. One of the best parts of the event is that a large amount of the faculty and staff turn out to serve the food and socialize with students.

Mr. Muhlenberg

During the spring semester, Muhlenberg holds a competition to see who will be crowned the next Mr. Muhlenberg. Several guys from each class year compete against each other in a variety of events such as swim wear, evening wear, and talent. Students vote for who they want to win by purchasing tickets for the event with their favorite guy's picture, and a board of students and faculty act as judges on the night of the event to choose who will win overall. While some may complain that it's sexist, it's a really entertaining night and everyone has a lot of fun participating.

Red Doors

As a sign of welcome, all of the doors on Muhlenberg's campus are painted bright red.

Through the Red Doors

Through the Red Doors is an event at the end of the spring semester that is run by Admissions for accepted students. A lot of current students enjoy participating in this day by serving on panels, giving tours, or representing different aspects of campus at tables during the information fair.

Finding a Job or Internship

The Lowdown On...
Finding a Job or Internship

Practically everyone in college is worried about finding a job or internship. Muhlenberg knows this and will do what they can to help you out. The Office of Career Development and Placement (OCDP) is a great resource, and they offer a number of services that will make the process of finding and applying to an internship or job run smoothly.

Advice

Don't hesitate to go to OCDP and find out more about how they can help you. Remember that they won't come to you! You will undoubtedly receive notices in your mailbox giving you information about upcoming workshops and other events, but it's up to you to actually attend these events. Also, talk to professors about where you'd be interested in working. They might have some advice or know people in the field who could be of help to you. Networking helps!

Career Center Resources & Services

Alumni in the Classroom Week

Career Campaign

Career Connections Online

Cover Letter Workshops

Dine for Success

Gearing Up for Graduate School Programs

Individual appointments with counselors

Internship database

Interview workshops

Job Search Strategies Workshop

Muhlenberg Career Network

Muhlenberg Shadow Program

Quick questions

Recruiting program

Resume critiques

Resume-O-Thon

Firms That Most Frequently Hire Graduates

AmeriCorps, Arbor Inc., AXA Advisors LLC, Baron Capital, Coca Cola, Deloitte & Touche LLP, Enterprise Rent-A-Car, Ernst & Young LLP, HCR Manor Care, Lord Abbett & Co., Mellon Financial Corp., Merrill Lynch, Muhlenberg College, PriceWaterhouseCoopers LLP, Salomon Smith Barney, St. Martin's Press, SEI Investments, Thomson Financial, UBS Paine Webber, Vangaurd Group, Wyeth Laboratories

Alumni

The Lowdown On...
Alumni

Web Site:
www.muhlenberg.edu/alumni

Office:
Muhlenberg College
Alumni Relations Office
2400 Chew St.
Allentown, PA 18104
bergalum@muhlenberg.edu
(800) 464-2374

Alumni Relations Office:
The Alumni Relations Office is located on the first floor to your left in the Haas College Center. The office is open 9 a.m.–5 p.m. on weekdays.

Services Available:
Alumni Insurance Services
Find a Friend
Regional Clubs
Message Boards

Alumni Publications

@ Muhlenberg Alumni Newsletter –
The newsletter is published on the Internet monthly at *www.muhlenberg.edu/alumni/newsletter/index.html.*

Muhlenberg Magazine –
This magazine is published quarterly, and it is free of charge. You can have it mailed to your house or check it out on the Web site: *www.muhlenberg.edu/cultural/magazine.*

Major Alumni Events

The main events for alumni are Homecoming and Reunion Weekend. Homecoming is typically in October and mainly focuses on the football game with a special lunch immediately before the game. Reunion Weekend is held in May, and there is a whole schedule of events for alumni from specific years.

Did You Know?

Famous Muhlenberg Alumni

Richard Ben-Viniste – Attorney, lead prosecutor in Watergate case

Frederick Busch – Author, Fairchild Professor of Literature at Colgate University

David Fricke – Senior editor for *Rolling Stone*

Robert David Steele – Author

Student Organizations

This is a sample list of the social and academic clubs available for students to join at Muhlenberg. For a full listing, visit the student organizations Web site at *www.muhlenberg.edu/studorgs/studorgslist.html*.

AcaFellas

Accounting Society

ACS Colleges Against Cancer

The Advocate (electronic newspaper)

Alpha Phi Omega

Alternative Spring Break Challenge Club

Anime Club

Anthropology and Sociology Club (ASC)

Art Association

Asian/International Students Association

Berg Organization Of Music (BOOM)

Best Buddies

Big Treble A Cappella

Biology Club

- Black Students Association
- Business & Economics Club
- Campus Christian Fellowship
- Cardinal Key Society
- Chai-monics A Capella
- Chemistry Club
- Chess Club
- Ciarla (yearbook)
- ClubWriters' Guild
- College Democrats
- College Libertarians
- College Republicans
- Communications Club
- Companion Club
- Computer Science Club
- Comunidad Latina
- Disability Awareness Club
- The Dynamics
- Education Society
- Emergency Medical Service (MCEMS)
- EnAcT (Environmental Action Team)
- Faith Works
- Flying Solo a capella
- Gaming Society
- Gay-Straight Alliance (GSA)
- Girls Next Door
- Habitat for Humanity
- HALO Club
- Hillel (Jewish)
- History Club
- International Students Association
- John Marshall Pre-Law Society
- Knit Wits
- Le Cercle Francais

Lutheran Student Movement
Math Club
Men Against Sexual Crimes (MASC)
Mint
Muhlenberg Activities Council (MAC)
Muhlenberg Alliance for Progressive Action (MAPA)
Muhlenberg College Campus Watch
Muhlenberg College TV (MCTV)
Muhlenberg Dance Association (MDA)
Muhlenberg Irish Cultural Society (MICS)
Muhlenberg Theatre Association (MTA)
Muhlenberg Weekly, The(student newspaper)
Muses Art and Literary Magazine
Newman Club (Catholic Campus Ministry)
The Newton Society
The Perkulators Dance Team
Philosophy Club
Psychology Club
R.I.B.B.O.N. Project
Residence Hall Association (RHA)
Russian Club
SEVEN
Sexual Assault Student Support (SASS)
Soul Sound Steppers
Spanish Club
Star-Crossed Students
Student Council
Students Advocating Gender Equality (SAGE)
Students Have a Real Effect (S.H.A.R.E.)
Synapse
Tour Guides
WMUH Allentown 91.7 FM
The Women in Business

The Best & Worst

The Ten **BEST** Things About Muhlenberg

1. Free entertainment and food in Seegers and on the lawn
2. Sense of community
3. Small student population
4. Professors
5. Desserts
6. Hanging out on the lawn on a nice day
7. Keeping your phone number and mailbox for all four years
8. Friendly staff
9. Variety of great musical and theatrical groups
10. Frisbee golf

The Ten WORST Things About Muhlenberg

1. Small student population
2. Lack of diversity
3. Garden Room on Friday and Sunday nights
4. Finding a parking spot
5. Waiting in line to register for classes
6. Parking tickets
7. Housing lottery
8. Library hours of operation
9. Minimal party scene
10. How much everything costs on campus

Visiting

The Lowdown On...
Visiting

Hotel Information:

Allentown Comfort Inn-Lehigh Valley West
7625 Imperial Way
Allentown, PA 18106
(610) 391-0344
www.comfortinn.com
Distance from Campus: 7 miles
Price Range: $69–$129

Best Western at the Gateway Conference Center
300 Gateway Dr.
Bethlehem, PA 18017
(610) 866-5800
www.bestwestern.com
Distance from Campus: 11 miles
Price Range: $89–$110

Comfort Suites of Allentown
3712 Hamilton Blvd.
Allentown, PA 18103
(610) 437-9100
www.comfortsuites.com
Distance from Campus:
2 miles
Price Range: $69–$119

Courtyard by Marriott
2160 Motel Dr.
Bethlehem, PA 18018
(610) 317-6200
www.marriott.com
Distance from Campus:
8 miles
Price Range: $89–$129

Crowne Plaza Allentown
904 Hamilton St.
Allentown, PA 18101
(610) 433-2221
www.crowneplaza.com
Distance from Campus:
2 miles
Price Range: $89–$159

Days Inn Conference Center
1151 Bulldog Dr.
Allentown, PA 18104
(610) 395-3731
www.daysinn.com
Distance from Campus:
4 miles
Price Range: $45–$130

Days Inn-Lehigh
2622 Lehigh St.
Allentown, PA 18103
(610) 797-1234
www.daysinn.com
Distance from Campus:
5 miles
Price Range: $59–$159

Glasbern Country Inn
2141, Pack House Rd.
Fogelsville, PA 18051
(610) 285-4723
www.glasbern.com
Distance from Campus:
10 miles
Price Range: $150–$446

Hampton Inn Allentown
7471 Keebler Way
Allentown, PA 18106
(610) 391-1500
www.hamptoninn.com
Distance from Campus:
9 miles
Price Range: $69–$169

Hampton Inn Quakertown
1915 John Fries Hwy.
Quakertown, PA 18951
(215) 536-7779
www.hamptoninn.com
Distance from Campus:
18 miles
Price Range: $99–$159

Hawthorn Suites
7720 Main St.
Fogelsville, PA 18051
(610) 366-9422
www.hawthorn.com
Distance from Campus:
8 miles
Price Range: $89–$140

Holiday Inn Conference Center
7736 Adrienne Dr.
Breinigsville, PA 18031
(610) 391-1000
www.holiday-inn.com
Distance from Campus:
8 miles
Price Range: $89–$129

Holiday Inn Express Allentown
3620 Hamilton Blvd.
Allentown, PA 18103
(610) 437-9255
www.hiexpress.com
Distance from Campus:
2 miles
Price Range: $65–$230

Holiday Inn Express Hotel & Suites
1918 John Fries Hwy.
Quakertown, PA 18951
(215) 529-7979
www.hiexpress.com
Distance from Campus:
18 miles
Price Range: $69–$140

Howard Johnson Inn and Suites
3220 Hamilton Blvd.
Allentown, PA 18103
(610) 439-4000
www.hojo.com
Distance from Campus:
2 miles
Price Range: $39–$129

Ramada Inn at the Malls
1500 Whitehall Rd.
Whitehall, PA 18052
(610) 439-1037
www.ramada.com
Distance from Campus:
5 miles
Price Range: $50–$150

Residence Inn by Marriott
2180 Motel Dr.
Bethlehem, PA 18018
(610) 317-2662
www.marriott.com
Distance from Campus:
8 miles
Price Range: $79–$124

Sheraton Hotel and Suites by Marriott
3400 Airport Rd.
Allentown, PA 18109
(610) 266-1000
www.sheraton.com
Distance from Campus:
9 miles
Price Range: $79–$179

Staybridge Suites Allentown
1787-A Airport Rd.
Allentown, PA 18109
(610) 443-5000
www.staybridge.com
Distance from Campus:
8 miles
Price Range: $99–$209

Take a Campus Virtual Tour

http://muhlenberg.edu/tour/index.html

To Schedule a Group Information Session or Interview

The admissions staff is available for interviews or information sessions by appointment Monday-Friday throughout the year and selected Saturdays from September through March.

Call (484) 664-3200 on any weekday from 9 a.m.–5 p.m.

Campus Tours

Campus tours are available on virtually every business day throughout the year and selected Saturdays in the fall and spring.

Call (484) 664-3200 for more information and schedule details.

Campus Visitation Program

The Campus Visitation Program is available for high school students wishing to spend time with Muhlenberg students and attend classes. This is a great opportunity to see what life on campus is really like. Students can spend a night in a dorm with a host or choose to just spend the day attending classes and meeting with a student for lunch. This service is available starting in the fall on Sunday through Thursday with the exception of holidays, breaks, and finals.

To schedule a visit, call (484) 664-3202.

Directions to Campus

Driving from the North

- Take the Northeast Extension of the Pennsylvania Turnpike (Route 476) south to Exit 56 (or old Exit 33), Lehigh Valley.
- Take Route 22 to Exit 55 (also marked Route 29), Cedar Crest Boulevard.
- Follow Cedar Crest Boulevard to the third traffic light.
- Turn left onto Chew Street, and bear right at the fork.
- Follow Chew Street for about one mile, and the campus will be on the left.

Driving from the South

- Take I-95 north to Philadelphia.
- When you enter Pennsylvania, take either the Walt Whitman Bridge or Ben Franklin Bridge to I-76, the Schuykill Expressway.
- Follow the Schuykill Expressway to the Turnpike (I-276) east to Route 476, the Northeast Extension (also known as the Blue Route).
- Take the Northeast Extension to Exit 56, the Lehigh Valley Exit.
- Take Route 22 east to Exit 55, Cedar Crest Boulevard.
- Follow Cedar Crest Boulevard to the third traffic light.
- Turn left onto Chew Street, and bear right at the fork.
- Follow Chew Street for about one mile, and the campus will be on the left.

Driving from the East

- Take I-78 West into Pennsylvania to Exit 55, Cedar Crest Boulevard.
- Take Cedar Crest Boulevard north approximately 2 miles towards Allentown.
- Turn right onto Chew Street, and bear right at the fork.
- Follow Chew Street for about one mile, and the campus will be on the left.

Driving from the West
- Take Route 81 to I-78 East.
- I-78 is shortly joined by Route 22.
- Take Route 22 to Exit 55 (also marked Route 29), Cedar Crest Boulevard.
- Follow Cedar Crest Boulevard to the third traffic light.
- Turn left onto Chew Street, and bear right at the fork.
- Follow Chew Street for about one mile, and the campus will be on the left.

Words to Know

Academic Probation – A suspension imposed on a student if he or she fails to keep up with the school's minimum academic requirements. Those unable to improve their grades after receiving this warning can face dismissal.

Beer Pong/Beirut – A drinking game involving cups of beer arranged in a pyramid shape on each side of a table. The goal is to get a ping pong ball into one of the opponent's cups by throwing the ball or hitting it with a paddle. If the ball lands in a cup, the opponent is required to drink the beer.

Bid – An invitation from a fraternity or sorority to 'pledge' (join) that specific house.

Blue-Light Phone – Brightly-colored phone posts with a blue light bulb on top. These phones exist for security purposes and are located at various outside locations around most campuses. In an emergency, a student can pick up one of these phones (free of charge) to connect with campus police or a security escort.

Campus Police – Police who are specifically assigned to a given institution. Campus police are typically not regular city officers; they are employed by the university in a full-time capacity.

Club Sports – A level of sports that falls somewhere between varsity and intramural. If a student is unable to commit to a varsity team but has a lot of passion for athletics, a club sport could be a better, less intense option. Even less demanding, intramural (IM) sports often involve no traveling and considerably less time.

Cocaine – An illegal drug. Also known as "coke" or "blow," cocaine often resembles a white crystalline or powdery substance. It is highly addictive and dangerous.

Common Application – An application with which students can apply to multiple schools.

Course Registration – The period of official class selection for the upcoming quarter or semester. Prior to registration, it is best to prepare several back-up courses in case a particular class becomes full. If a course is full, students can place themselves on the waitlist, although this still does not guarantee entry.

Division Athletics – Athletic classifications range from Division I to Division III. Division IA is the most competitive, while Division III is considered to be the least competitive.

Dorm – A dorm (or dormitory) is an on-campus housing facility. Dorms can provide a range of options from suite-style rooms to more communal options that include shared bathrooms. Most first-year students live in dorms. Some upperclassmen who wish to stay on campus also choose this option.

Early Action – An application option with which a student can apply to a school and receive an early acceptance response without a binding commitment. This system is becoming less and less available.

Early Decision – An application option that students should use only if they are certain they plan to attend the school in question. If a student applies using the early decision option and is admitted, he or she is required and bound to attend that university. Admission rates are usually higher among students who apply through early decision, as the student is clearly indicating that the school is his or her first choice.

Ecstasy – An illegal drug. Also known as "E" or "X," ecstasy looks like a pill and most resembles an aspirin. Considered a party drug, ecstasy is very dangerous and can be deadly.

Ethernet – An extremely fast Internet connection available in most university-owned residence halls. To use an Ethernet connection properly, a student will need a network card and cable for his or her computer.

Fake ID – A counterfeit identification card that contains false information. Most commonly, students get fake IDs with altered birthdates so that they appear to be older than 21 (and therefore of legal drinking age). Even though it is illegal, many college students have fake IDs in hopes of purchasing alcohol or getting into bars.

Frosh – Slang for "freshman" or "freshmen."

Hazing – Initiation rituals administered by some fraternities or sororities as part of the pledging process. Many universities have outlawed hazing due to its degrading, and sometimes dangerous, nature.

Intramurals (IMs) – A popular, and usually free, sport league in which students create teams and compete against one another. These sports vary in competitiveness and can include a range of activities—everything from billiards to water polo. IM sports are a great way to meet people with similar interests.

Keg – Officially called a half-barrel, a keg contains roughly 200 12-ounce servings of beer.

LSD – An illegal drug, also known as acid, this hallucinogenic drug most commonly resembles a tab of paper.

Marijuana – An illegal drug, also known as weed or pot; along with alcohol, marijuana is one of the most commonly-found drugs on campuses across the country.

Major –The focal point of a student's college studies; a specific topic that is studied for a degree. Examples of majors include physics, English, history, computer science, economics, business, and music. Many students decide on a specific major before arriving on campus, while others are simply "undecided" until declaring a major. Those who are extremely interested in two areas can also choose to double major.

Meal Block – The equivalent of one meal. Students on a meal plan usually receive a fixed number of meals per week. Each meal, or "block," can be redeemed at the school's dining facilities in place of cash. Often, a student's weekly allotment of meal blocks will be forfeited if not used.

Minor – An additional focal point in a student's education. Often serving as a complement or addition to a student's main area of focus, a minor has fewer requirements and prerequisites to fulfill than a major. Minors are not required for graduation from most schools; however some students who want to explore many different interests choose to pursue both a major and a minor.

Mushrooms – An illegal drug. Also known as "'shrooms," this drug resembles regular mushrooms but is extremely hallucinogenic.

Off-Campus Housing – Housing from a particular landlord or rental group that is not affiliated with the university. Depending on the college, off-campus housing can range from extremely popular to non-existent. Students who choose to live off campus are typically given more freedom, but they also have to deal with possible subletting scenarios, furniture, bills, and other issues. In addition to these factors, rental prices and distance often affect a student's decision to move off campus.

Office Hours – Time that teachers set aside for students who have questions about coursework. Office hours are a good forum for students to go over any problems and to show interest in the subject material.

Pledging – The early phase of joining a fraternity or sorority, pledging takes place after a student has gone through rush and received a bid. Pledging usually lasts between one and two semesters. Once the pledging period is complete and a particular student has done everything that is required to become a member, that student is considered a brother or sister. If a fraternity or a sorority would decide to "haze" a group of students, this initiation would take place during the pledging period.

Private Institution – A school that does not use tax revenue to subsidize education costs. Private schools typically cost more than public schools and are usually smaller.

Prof – Slang for "professor."

Public Institution – A school that uses tax revenue to subsidize education costs. Public schools are often a good value for in-state residents and tend to be larger than most private colleges.

Quarter System (or Trimester System) – A type of academic calendar system. In this setup, students take classes for three academic periods. The first quarter usually starts in late September or early October and concludes right before Christmas. The second quarter usually starts around early to mid–January and finishes up around March or April. The last academic quarter, or "third quarter," usually starts in late March or early April and finishes up in late May or Mid-June. The fourth quarter is summer. The major difference between the quarter system and semester system is that students take more, less comprehensive courses under the quarter calendar.

RA (Resident Assistant) – A student leader who is assigned to a particular floor in a dormitory in order to help to the other students who live there. An RA's duties include ensuring student safety and providing assistance wherever possible.

Recitation – An extension of a specific course; a review session. Some classes, particularly large lectures, are supplemented with mandatory recitation sessions that provide a relatively personal class setting.

Rolling Admissions – A form of admissions. Most commonly found at public institutions, schools with this type of policy continue to accept students throughout the year until their class sizes are met. For example, some schools begin accepting students as early as December and will continue to do so until April or May.

Room and Board – This figure is typically the combined cost of a university-owned room and a meal plan.

Room Draw/Housing Lottery – A common way to pick on-campus room assignments for the following year. If a student decides to remain in university-owned housing, he or she is assigned a unique number that, along with seniority, is used to determine his or her housing for the next year.

Rush – The period in which students can meet the brothers and sisters of a particular chapter and find out if a given fraternity or sorority is right for them. Rushing a fraternity or a sorority is not a requirement at any school. The goal of rush is to give students who are serious about pledging a feel for what to expect.

Semester System – The most common type of academic calendar system at college campuses. This setup typically includes two semesters in a given school year. The fall semester starts around the end of August or early September and concludes before winter vacation. The spring semester usually starts in mid-January and ends in late April or May.

Student Center/Rec Center/Student Union – A common area on campus that often contains study areas, recreation facilities, and eateries. This building is often a good place to meet up with fellow students; depending on the school, the student center can have a huge role or a non-existent role in campus life.

Student ID – A university-issued photo ID that serves as a student's key to school-related functions. Some schools require students to show these cards in order to get into dorms, libraries, cafeterias, and other facilities. In addition to storing meal plan information, in some cases, a student ID can actually work as a debit card and allow students to purchase things from bookstores or local shops.

Suite – A type of dorm room. Unlike dorms that feature communal bathrooms shared by the entire floor, suites offer bathrooms shared only among the suite. Suite-style dorm rooms can house anywhere from two to ten students.

TA (Teacher's Assistant) – An undergraduate or grad student who helps in some manner with a specific course. In some cases, a TA will teach a class, assist a professor, grade assignments, or conduct office hours.

Undergraduate – A student in the process of studying for his or her bachelor's degree.

ABOUT THE AUTHOR

I really enjoyed writing this book! This was a great experience that allowed me to express myself through my writing while learning a lot of interesting things about my college. I am currently a senior at Muhlenberg College where I am a Communication major and a Studio Art minor. After earning my degree, I look forward to pursuing a career that will allow me to make the most of what I have learned in both of these fields. My years at the 'Berg have been full of experiences that will make graduating and leaving very difficult. You can't fully anticipate these experiences just from reading a book, but I hope that this book has been both fun and helpful in providing you with insightful knowledge of Muhlenberg. I wish you the best of luck in your college search! If you have any questions or comments, don't hesitate to contact me at michellehein@collegeprowler.com.

Enough about me; I'd like to turn the spotlight onto the people that gave me support, advice, helpful tidbits, and laughs while writing this book. Many thanks to my family and friends; students and faculty who responded during their busy summers; the Admissions student-workers; and College Prowler for giving me this opportunity.

Michelle Hein
michellehein@collegeprowler.com

The College Prowler Big Book of Colleges

Having Trouble Narrowing Down Your Choices?
Try Going Bigger!

BIG BOOK OF COLLEGES '09
7¼" X 10", 1248 Pages Paperback
$29.95 Retail
978-1-4274-0005-5

Choosing the perfect school can be an overwhelming challenge. Luckily, our *Big Book of Colleges* makes that task a little less daunting. We've packed it with overviews of our full library of single-school guides—more than 280 of the nation's top schools—giving you some much-needed perspective on your search.

College Prowler on the Web

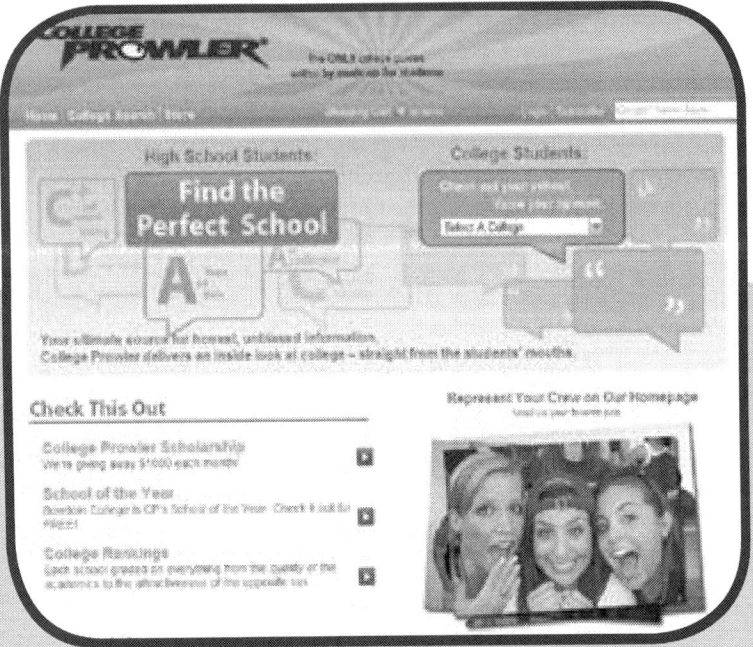

Craving some electronic interaction? Check out the new and improved **CollegeProwler.com**! We've included the COMPLETE contents of more than 250 of our single-school guides on the Web—and you can gain access to all of them for just $39.95 per year!

Not only that, but non-subscribers can still view and compare our grades for each school, order books at our online bookstore, or enter our monthly scholarship contest. Don't get left in the dark when making your college decision. Let College Prowler be your guide!

Get the Jolt!

College Jolt gives you a peek behind the scenes

College Jolt is our new blog designed to hook you up with great information, funny videos, cool contests, awesome scholarship opportunities, and honest insight into who we are and what we're all about.

Check us out at ***www.collegejolt.com***

Need Help Paying For School?
Apply for our scholarship!

College Prowler awards thousands of dollars a year to students who compose the best essays. E-mail scholarship@collegeprowler.com for more information, or call 1-800-290-2682.

Apply now at **www.collegeprowler.com**

Tell Us What Life Is Really Like at Your School!

Have you ever wanted to let people know what your college is really like? Now's your chance to help millions of high school students choose the right college.

Let your voice be heard.

Check out **www.collegeprowler.com** for more info!

Need More Help?

Do you have more questions about this school? Can't find a certain statistic? College Prowler is here to help. We are the best source of college information out there. We have a network of thousands of students who can get the latest information on any school to you ASAP. E-mail us at info@collegeprowler.com with your college-related questions.

E-Mail Us Your College-Related Questions!

Check out **www.collegeprowler.com** for more details.
1-800-290-2682

Write For Us!
Get published! Voice your opinion.

Writing a College Prowler guidebook is both fun and rewarding; our open-ended format allows your own creativity free reign. Our writers have been featured in national newspapers and have seen their names in bookstores across the country. Now is your chance to break into the publishing industry with one of the country's fastest-growing publishers!

Apply now at ***www.collegeprowler.com***

Contact editor@collegeprowler.com or call 1-800-290-2682 for more details.

Pros and Cons

Still can't figure out if this is the right school for you? You've already read through this in-depth guide; why not list the pros and cons? It will really help with narrowing down your decision and determining whether or not this school is right for you.

Pros	**Cons**
....	....
....	....
....	....
....	....
....	....
....	....
....	....
....	....
....	....
....	....
....	....
....	....
....	....

Pros and Cons

Still can't figure out if this is the right school for you?
You've already read through this in-depth guide;
why not list the pros and cons? It will really help
with narrowing down your decision and determining
whether or not this school is right for you.

Pros	**Cons**
....	....
....	....
....	....
....	....
....	....
....	....
....	....
....	....
....	....
....	....
....	....
....	....
....	....

Notes

Notes

Notes

Notes

Notes

Notes

Notes

Notes

Notes

Notes

Notes

Notes

Notes

Notes

Notes

Notes

Notes

Notes

Notes

Notes

Notes

Notes

Notes

Notes

Order now! • collegeprowler.com • 1.800.290.2682
Over 260 single-school guidebooks!

Albion College
Alfred University
Allegheny College
American University
Amherst College
Arizona State University
Auburn University
Babson College
Ball State University
Bard College
Barnard College
Bates College
Baylor University
Beloit College
Bentley College
Binghamton University
Birmingham Southern College
Boston College
Boston University
Bowdoin College
Brandeis University
Brigham Young University
Brown University
Bryn Mawr College
Bucknell University
Cal Poly
Cal Poly Pomona
Cal State Northridge
Cal State Sacramento
Caltech
Carleton College
Carnegie Mellon University
Case Western Reserve
Centenary College of Louisiana
Centre College
Claremont McKenna College
Clark Atlanta University
Clark University
Clemson University
Colby College
Colgate University
College of Charleston
College of the Holy Cross
College of William & Mary
College of Wooster
Colorado College
Columbia University
Connecticut College
Cornell University
Creighton University
CUNY Hunters College
Dartmouth College
Davidson College
Denison University
DePauw University
Dickinson College
Drexel University
Duke University
Duquesne University
Earlham College
East Carolina University
Elon University
Emerson College
Emory University
FIT
Florida State University
Fordham University

Franklin & Marshall College
Furman University
Geneva College
George Washington University
Georgetown University
Georgia Tech
Gettysburg College
Gonzaga University
Goucher College
Grinnell College
Grove City College
Guilford College
Gustavus Adolphus College
Hamilton College
Hampshire College
Hampton University
Hanover College
Harvard University
Harvey Mudd College
Haverford College
Hofstra University
Hollins University
Howard University
Idaho State University
Illinois State University
Illinois Wesleyan University
Indiana University
Iowa State University
Ithaca College
IUPUI
James Madison University
Johns Hopkins University
Juniata College
Kansas State
Kent State University
Kenyon College
Lafayette College
LaRoche College
Lawrence University
Lehigh University
Lewis & Clark College
Louisiana State University
Loyola College in Maryland
Loyola Marymount University
Loyola University Chicago
Loyola University New Orleans
Macalester College
Marlboro College
Marquette University
McGill University
Miami University of Ohio
Michigan State University
Middle Tennessee State
Middlebury College
Millsaps College
MIT
Montana State University
Mount Holyoke College
Muhlenberg College
New York University
North Carolina State
Northeastern University
Northern Arizona University
Northern Illinois University
Northwestern University
Oberlin College
Occidental College

Ohio State University
Ohio University
Ohio Wesleyan University
Old Dominion University
Penn State University
Pepperdine University
Pitzer College
Pomona College
Princeton University
Providence College
Purdue University
Reed College
Rensselaer Polytechnic Institute
Rhode Island School of Design
Rhodes College
Rice University
Rochester Institute of Technology
Rollins College
Rutgers University
San Diego State University
Santa Clara University
Sarah Lawrence College
Scripps College
Seattle University
Seton Hall University
Simmons College
Skidmore College
Slippery Rock
Smith College
Southern Methodist University
Southwestern University
Spelman College
St. Joseph's University Philadelphia
St. John's University
St. Louis University
St. Olaf College
Stanford University
Stetson University
Stony Brook University
Susquhanna University
Swarthmore College
Syracuse University
Temple University
Tennessee State University
Texas A & M University
Texas Christian University
Towson University
Trinity College Connecticut
Trinity University Texas
Truman State
Tufts University
Tulane University
UC Berkeley
UC Davis
UC Irvine
UC Riverside
UC San Diego
UC Santa Barbara
UC Santa Cruz
UCLA
Union College
University at Albany
University at Buffalo
University of Alabama
University of Arizona
University of Central Florida
University of Chicago

University of Colorado
University of Connecticut
University of Delaware
University of Denver
University of Florida
University of Georgia
University of Illinois
University of Iowa
University of Kansas
University of Kentucky
University of Maine
University of Maryland
University of Massachusetts
University of Miami
University of Michigan
University of Minnesota
University of Mississippi
University of Missouri
University of Nebraska
University of New Hampshire
University of North Carolina
University of Notre Dame
University of Oklahoma
University of Oregon
University of Pennsylvania
University of Pittsburgh
University of Puget Sound
University of Rhode Island
University of Richmond
University of Rochester
University of San Diego
University of San Francisco
University of South Carolina
University of South Dakota
University of South Florida
University of Southern California
University of Tennessee
University of Texas
University of Utah
University of Vermont
University of Virginia
University of Washington
University of Wisconsin
UNLV
Ursinus College
Valparaiso University
Vanderbilt University
Vassar College
Villanova University
Virginia Tech
Wake Forest University
Warren Wilson College
Washington and Lee University
Washington University in St. Louis
Wellesley College
Wesleyan University
West Point
West Virginia University
Wheaton College IL.
Wheaton College MA
Whitman College
Wilkes University
Williams College
Xavier University
Yale University

Made in the USA
Lexington, KY
25 March 2010